Jesus Christ The Prince of preachers

Learning from the teaching ministry of Jesus

Foreword by John MacArthur

Mike Abendroth

DayOne

© Day One Publications 2008
First printed 2008

ISBN 978–1–84625–108–5

British Library Cataloguing in Publication Data available

Published by Day One Publications
Ryelands Road, Leominster, HR6 8NZ
☎ 01568 613 740 FAX 01568 611 473
email—sales@dayone.co.uk
web site—www.dayone.co.uk
North American—e-mail—sales@dayonebookstore.com
North American—web site—www.dayonebookstore.com

Cover design by Wayne McMaster
Printed in Canada

The greatest preacher of the written Word is, undoubtedly, the living Word Himself, the Lord Jesus Christ. If we are commanded to walk as He walked, then surely we must preach as He preached. This is the central thrust of this well-developed book. This work addresses what is surely the greatest need in the church today. It is not merely more preaching that is needed, but more preaching of a certain expository kind, especially the kind demonstrated by the sovereign Head of the church, Jesus Christ. Abendroth takes great care to lay out the case that all preachers should model themselves after the ministry of the Lord Jesus Himself. If there was more preaching as this book calls for, the church would soon be restored to a state of sound spiritual health. Here is a book that is biblical, balanced, and bold in its presentation of truth. Read it and replicate it for the equipping of your ministry and the edification of the church.

Dr Steven J. Lawson, Senior Pastor, Christ Fellowship Baptist Church, Mobile, Alabama, USA

I cannot imagine a preacher who would not be helped by this book. Mike Abendroth writes from years of local church pulpit ministry combined with a wide reading of books about preaching to produce a volume that is insightful, instructive, encouraging, practical, readable, and biblically sound. He delivers exactly what his subtitle promises: "Learning from the teaching ministry of Jesus." But Abendroth delivers even more than he promises, for readers will learn a great deal not only about Christ and preaching, but also about pastoral ministry, discipleship, worship, and much more. And he does it all in an imaginative format that is accessible for everyone. If you are a preacher, read this book. If you are not a preacher, read it, and then give it to your preacher.

Dr Donald Whitney, Associate Professor of Biblical Spirituality and Senior Associate Dean at The Southern Baptist Theological Seminary in Louisville, Kentucky

Bullseye! Right on the mark! What a joy to read a book on preaching that truly needed to be written and needs to be read. In his book Jesus Christ: The Prince of Preachers, Mike Abendroth provides an arsenal of insight to correct what is wrong, essentially, with preaching today. Each chapter makes a corrective contribution in an eightfold solution for the near pandemic of perilous preaching emitted from the typical pulpit that approaches treason against the God of the Word and treachery against the Word of God.

Commendations

This book offers a wealth of information that provides an insightful rethinking of the role and responsibility that preaching must have in the church of the Lord Jesus Christ. The format of the book is exceptional, providing insight to the preacher and those who hear preaching. The content of each chapter is choice material.

Jesus Christ: The Prince of Preachers *is not only a must-read book, but also one that should be reread annually. If only one book on preaching is to be purchased this year, buy this one! It may very well be the best investment you make this year. Abendroth has produced the most captivating book on preaching I have read in a long time. You will be challenged, equipped, and encouraged as you read it.*

Ben Awbrey, Th.D., Associate Professor of Preaching, Midwestern Baptist Theological Seminary, Kansas City, Missouri

What you win them with is what you win them to. Preaching is God's way of proclaiming the foolishness of the gospel to the weak and despised, all to His own glory. The world will always despise preaching, but when the church likewise questions God's wisdom and starts using alternatives, a major problem exists. Abendroth calls his readers back to the preeminence of preaching through the example of the Lord Himself. Encouraging and challenging.

James White, author of Scripture Alone, Pulpit Crimes, The God Who Justifies, and The King James Only Controversy

I have many books on preaching. Not one of them is like this one. Packed with truth which every preacher needs to know, full of brilliant insights into the preaching ministry of Jesus Christ, and enough to revitalize preaching from the perfect example of Jesus Christ, this book is one that I will recommend and promote whenever and wherever I can. It is bound to make its mark on the lives of preachers who read it and then, through them, on entire congregations when they listen to the kind preaching of that is taught by Mike Abendroth.

Martin Holdt, Minister of Constantia Park Baptist Church, Pretoria, and Rector of the Afrikaans Baptist Seminary, Kempton Park, South Africa

Biblical, theological and practical—these words capture the content of this book. Mike Abendroth provides a wealth of wisdom as he examines the greatest preacher ever to preach: the Lord Jesus Christ. I was challenged, instructed and encouraged by this work. Read it yourself, and I believe you too will be blessed.

Danny Akin, President, Southeastern Baptist Theological Seminary, Wake Forest, North Carolina

Every biblical preacher intuitively holds the Lord Jesus as his model for preaching but few of us have ever studied Jesus the Preacher. Mike Abendroth has done us all a big favor by presenting to us a thorough portrait of Jesus as the model expositor of Scripture. In Jesus Christ: the Prince of Preachers we have a scholarly, insightful, motivational, and practical tool in helping us preach the way the Preacher of preachers preached. Each chapter contains three sections of great usefulness. First, there is a study of a certain facet of our Lord's preaching; then, there is a section for the preacher on making use of the material covered; finally, there is a section for the congregation or layman to respond to the model presented.

It is evident that Mike Abendroth is a preacher, that he loves to preach, and loves the church of Christ. His style is warm, energetic, pointed, and convincing. His passion for the Word of God and for the need for sound preaching today is evident right from the first sentence. He wants us to move on from "What would Jesus do?" (WWJD) to "What would Jesus preach?" (WWJP).

Here is a dimension of the preacher's preparation that is rarely seen in books on preaching or taught in homiletical classrooms. You will be greatly rewarded for reading it.

I highly recommend Jesus Christ: the Prince of Preachers as a tool to help us become more like our Lord Jesus, the Preacher.

Alex D. Montoya, Professor of Pastoral Ministries, The Master's Seminary

The most compelling advice to any preacher is this: "Preach as Jesus preached." But what does that really mean? Mike Abendroth has answered this question with a fresh

Commendations

and fascinating analysis of Jesus' preaching in Jesus Christ: The Prince of Preachers. These pages are an irresistible invitation to imitate the style and substance of the greatest teacher ever.

Rick Holland, Senior Associate Pastor, Grace Community Church, Director of D.Min. Studies, The Master's Seminary

Abendroth's insightful work is so helpful, calling Christians today to consider the model of the Master Teacher Himself. Thoroughly biblical and intensely practical, this Christ-centered treatment on preaching deserves a place on every pastor's bookshelf. In a day when so many pulpits are less than weak, it is a timely and necessary challenge to those who are called to "preach the Word" (2 Tim. 4:2). But this book is not only for those in church leadership. It also articulates what each congregation should expect from their teaching pastor, as they lovingly hold him to the standard set by our Lord.

John MacArthur, Pastor-Teacher, Grace Community Church, Sun Valley, California

"[Jesus] alone is the Prince of preachers.

He alone is the best of expositors."

Thomas Watson

Dedication

To my children, Hayley, Luke, Maddie, and Grace. May all the preachers you listen to preach like Jesus Christ. You have greatly encouraged your father as he preached to you at the family dinner table. May your love for Jesus Christ and His preaching increase!

Trying to be succinct in acknowledging encouragement, assistance, and guidance is a very difficult undertaking. To begin with, I am the blessed recipient of God's grace and God's grace alone. Thankfully, the Lord has ordained the use of other Christians to sanctify and assist His people. In other words, I understand that He uses other Christians as channels of His grace. I praise the Lord for all the help He has given me for this project.

Furthermore, the truths contained in this book are far from original. They are truths that I have learned and gleaned from others. I then "Abendroth-ized" them through my own life experiences and personality. I take complete responsibility for any error in the translation.

The saints at Bethlehem Bible Church, West Boylston, Massachusetts, are a loving and faithful flock. You are a blessing to me. I rejoice because of you and your patience over the past ten years as I have strived, and continue to strive, to preach more as Christ preached. I love you for many reasons, but one is that you love expository preaching that exalts Jesus Christ.

I thank my fellow elders at Bethlehem Bible Church: Steve Cooley, Dave Jeffries, Louis Brown, and Pradeep Tilak. These men are models of 1 Timothy 3:1–7 and have encouraged this book from start to finish. What a privilege it is to serve with men like you—men committed to guarding God's honor!

Thanks to Sheryl Caissie for her help in editing, flow, and writing. Thank you for your encouragement to see Christ's church experience preaching that echoes that of Christ Jesus Himself.

To the men in my "preaching-discipleship" classes: thank you for putting up with my strange techniques in discipleship (preaching to the tombstones in the wee hours of the morning and enduring "scare tactics" such as the Russian National Anthem), for assisting me in the crystallization of ideas for discipling men to teach the Bible, and for persevering through hermeneutics and exegesis classes.

I am grateful to Tracy Johansen for her persistence in tracking down quotes, books, and references.

Day One has been a pleasure to work with from start to finish. Jim Holmes, thanks for your ideas, encouragement, and vision for this project.

Ackowledgements

I have never worked with a publisher before, but you have set the standard for godliness. I have appreciated your Christlike attitude in your "job." May everyone work for the Lord's glory as you do!

Suzanne Mitchell took my manuscript and ran with it. Thank you, Suzanne, for your keen eye, excellent diction and grammar, and quick work. I would be lost without you.

John MacArthur's ministry in my life has been life-changing on so many levels. If the word "cataclysmic" can denote something positive and good, then John's life has had a cataclysmic effect on my life. Thank you, John, for your consistent modeling of expository proclamation that so closely resembles the preaching of Jesus Christ. When I think of the thousands of preachers that God has raised up over the centuries, I truly praise Him for allowing me to sit under a preacher like you. You are my spiritual father in every way, shape, and form. Your Foreword is humbling and demonstrates the Lord's great working through fragile vessels.

I am in debt to the positive and constructive influences of Alex Montoya, Ben Awbrey, and Danny Akin. These professors of homiletics at The Master's Seminary and Southern Baptist Theological Seminary challenged me in every area.

Last, but not least, I am grateful for my bride of eighteen years, Kimberly. You are the best of the best. I had no idea what I was getting into when I married you, but the Lord did and He granted me my most precious gift outside of salvation. Thanks for being my soul mate, friend, and co-laborer for the Preacher of preachers.

No task in ministry is more important than preaching. It is the God-ordained means by which His truth is communicated to His people. Not surprisingly, many of the most familiar names in the Bible—including Enoch, Noah, Moses, Elijah, Isaiah, Jeremiah, Ezra, John the Baptist, Peter, Paul, and Timothy—were preachers. Though generally unpopular in their own day, they were powerful men of God, used by Him to faithfully deliver His message to the world. They were notable men, "men of whom the world was not worthy" (Hebrews 11:38), and their legacy continues even to the present.

But of all the great preachers, in both Scripture and church history, none compares to the true Prince of preachers, Jesus Christ. He not only preached a divine message, but He did so with inherent divine authority as the incarnate Word of God. When He taught, the people were astonished at the power and precision of His words. His wisdom was unprecedented; His influence unsurpassed; and His compassion as unmistakable as His zeal and authority. He superseded all who came before His incarnation and all who have come after, for, as God in human flesh, He is the very standard by which preaching could ever possibly be measured.

There are, of course, certain limits on how far we can imitate Jesus' preaching. He lived a sinless and perfect life; we are fallen and depraved. He claimed to be the Son of God; we claim to be nothing more than mere men. He proclaimed salvation and forgiveness through Himself; we proclaim salvation and forgiveness not through ourselves but through Him. He spoke with divine authority because He is God; we speak with divine authority only when we proclaim what God has already revealed. He performed unique miracles to authenticate His message; we perform nothing of the sort. For those who know and love Him, Jesus Christ is not merely a model of preaching, He is the glorious object of our preaching and the absolute sovereign of our pulpits.

At the same time, the Lord *did* model many things that the contemporary preacher can and should emulate. The scriptural content of His gospel message; the holy compassion of His interaction with sinners; the uncompromising resolve of His confrontations with the Pharisees; the humble prayerfulness of His preparation; the unyielding boldness of His proclamation; the piercing precision of His application; and the overarching concern for God's glory that blanketed everything He said and did—these are all areas in which today's expositor can learn a great deal. They are also areas in which the contemporary church has fallen woefully short.

It is here that Abendroth's insightful work is so helpful, calling Christians today to consider the model of the Master Teacher Himself. Thoroughly biblical and intensely practical, this Christ-centered treatment on preaching deserves a place on every pastor's bookshelf. In a day when so many pulpits are less than weak, it is a timely and necessary challenge to those who are called to "preach the word" (2 Timothy 4:2). But this book is not only for those in church leadership: it also articulates what members of every congregation should expect from their teaching pastor, as they lovingly hold him to the standard set by our Lord.

So many churches need to be reminded about what real preaching looks like. In an effort to be "relevant," countless congregations have exchanged expository preaching for seeker-driven programs; doctrinal accuracy for postmodern ambiguity; and biblical precision for cultural popularity. But in so doing, they have strayed from the model given by Jesus Christ. He did not tickle ears. He did not water down the gospel. He did not capitulate. Instead, He spoke the truth with boldness, conviction, and authority. May those who represent Him, as His undershepherds, be faithful to do the same.

Contents

Triage. Triage is the method of prioritizing the severity of medical victims in an emergency situation, so that the most critical patients receive care first. Triage attempts to guarantee the most efficient use of the doctors, nurses, and medical facilities; it answers the question, "Who gets attention first?"

Ecclesiological triage. The professing evangelical church is in a state of emergency. She is alive, but very sick. The health of the church today is in trouble, in spite of swelling numbers, mega-buildings, and expanding "borders." She has been in a head-on collision with the eighteen-wheel semi-truck of postmodernity. The problems are so large and plentiful, nothing less than ecclesiological triage will sift through the myriad of problems and begin to lend spiritual attention to the top priorities. Sadly, triage procedures leave some patients to die, since the best staff make the decision that these patients are beyond assistance and will die even if they receive emergency treatment. What remedy for the evangelical church is most needed? What needs to be done immediately while we leave other problems, real or imagined, untouched?

We must preach, and we must do so as Jesus, the Prince of preachers, did. We must also measure excellence in preaching by comparing all preachers to Jesus Himself.

The ultimate priority for the revived church is preaching. The pulpit lies at the heart of the church. Preaching pumps the lifeblood of God's Word into the arteries, veins, and capillaries of the local church's vital organs. Walter Kaiser knows why the church is languishing, and he understands the solution to the problem, saying,

It is no secret that Christ's Church is not at all in good health in many places of the world. She has been languishing because she has been fed ... "junk food" ... The Biblical text is often no more than a slogan or refrain in the message ... Biblical exposition has become a lost art in contemporary preaching ... American parishioners ... are often rewarded with more or less of the same treatment: repetitious arrangements of the most elementary truths of the faith ... Where is that sense of authority and mission previously associated with the Biblical Word?[1]

The church has exchanged her preaching birthright for a watered-down stew of PowerPoint presentations, drama, methods, slide shows, movie clips, felt needs, psychology, techniques, and programs that are designed to fill the pews. This "stew" will not fill the person in the pew with hygienic, sound, meaty doctrine, which is critical for healthy Christian living. We need men at our sacred desks today who will not apologize for cutting the Word of truth straightly, in context, with boldness, directed at the heart, and carefully exegeted. The world may deem these men of God "dinosaurs," "obscurantists," "sheltered," "cave dwellers," or "troglodytes," but the Judge of the living and of the dead will call them "blessed" and "obedient servants."

Preaching is the issue, not just any kind of preaching, but preaching that will rescue the lethargic church. It is the premise of this book that, if pastors would preach as Jesus did, their churches would flourish spiritually and God would be honored. If laypeople and congregations would rise up and demand Christ-like preaching from their pulpits, the church would immediately begin to shake off her lethargy and start on the path of full recovery. She would then begin to reach out with evangelism, because healthy sheep reproduce.

Jesus the preacher needs close examination and investigation so that Christian preachers see His greatness and yearn to preach like Him.

It seems obvious, yet modern Christian publishing effectively ignores the concept of preaching as Jesus preached. During my doctoral work in expository preaching, I read a plethora of books on preaching—expository preaching, redemptive-historical preaching—yet the books that focused on Jesus' preaching style were rare or nonexistent.

I could prove my point this way: You probably have your favorite books on preaching. Here is my challenge: Would your top ten books on preaching each contain, at a minimum, one chapter on training the student to learn from Jesus and His preaching? Would there be at least one chapter in all those books in total? Sadly, this topic is so assumed in preaching that it is often overlooked and under-applied. This should strike the reader strangely! I did some quick research. I have sixty-six evangelical books on preaching (and more liberal ones that I didn't count). These sixty-six books contain a total of 842 chapters. Ironically, only four of those chapters deal with "Jesus the preacher" or something similar. I did find three books devoted exclusively to Jesus and His preaching, but these were dated, more liberal, and did not offer much for students today.

E.C. Dargan describes the drought of books about Jesus and His homiletics—although he wrote about one hundred years ago, Dargan sounds like he is analyzing books about modern preaching—"In the vast literature in which every aspect of the life and work of Jesus has been presented it is remarkable that, comparatively, so little appears on the subject of this volume ... the preaching of Jesus, as preaching, finds illuminating and helpful discussion; but the study is incidental and limited, not exclusive and elaborate."[2] Albert Bond knew the same thing E.C. Dargan knew: "While the ministry of Jesus has had large attention from scholars as to the questions of biblical theology, there has not been published any adequate treatment of that ministry from the viewpoint of homiletics. Jesus was distinctively the Master Preacher, but his preaching, as preaching, has been neglected."[3]

Purpose

Again, the purpose of this book is to make explicit what all Christian homileticians know implicitly, that is, that there is much to learn from Jesus as we examine His style of preaching and what He preached. It is not as simple as "WWJD" ("What would Jesus do?"); nevertheless, there are plenty of opportunities in the Gospels to study the Master Preacher with an eye toward emulation.[4]

After closely studying the Sermon on the Mount in Matthew 5–7, it dawned on me, with an epiphany-like force, that the sermons and style of Jesus should influence all preachers and congregations. Pastors should love to preach like Jesus did, and laypeople should love to hear preaching that reflects the way Jesus preached. While many new books give the clarion call to preach Christ in all sermons, avoid moralizing, focus on the redemptive story of Christ, and preach Christ from the Old Testament (all good things), I call every reader of this book to look to Christ and study Him as the true "Prince of all preachers" (sorry, Spurgeon).

Jesus is known by many rich and wonderful titles: Savior, Lord, Messiah, King, Judge, Son of God, Son of Man, Alpha and Omega, Holy

One, Lamb, Advocate, Author, Finisher, Captain, Lion, Mediator, Prophet, Shepherd, Redeemer, Emmanuel, Ancient of Days, The Angel of the Lord, The Word, The First and the Last, and many more. But this book wants you to also think of Him as PREACHER! Jesus the Preacher. Thomas Watson, the Puritan writer, thought of Jesus in this manner:

He alone is the Prince of Preachers. He alone is the best of expositors ... The One in whom there was a combination of virtues; a constellation of beauties, the One in whose lips there was not only sweet as honeycomb, but His very words did drop as honeycomb. His words were an oracle, His works were a miracle, His life was a pattern, His death was a sacrifice, and it was He, that blessed Man, who went up into this mountain and sat down and spake unto His disciples.[5]

It behooves Christians to get the microscope out and revel in the wonderful preaching of the Savior.

Format

Each chapter contains three sections. The first section is a brief exposition from a Gospel. I will attempt to show how Jesus did what the title of each chapter suggests.

The next two sections will bring to bear the truth taught in the first section. The second section will be devoted to the practical implications of Jesus' preaching for pastors, preachers, leaders, elders, and all who teach the Bible formally or informally. The third section will challenge people who regularly listen to preaching. Laypeople and congregations must see the importance of listening to preaching in a way that would honor Jesus. They should hear the Word taught as if they are actually listening to Him preach. These sections at the end of each chapter are intended to promote Erasmus' slogan: "If elephants can be trained to dance, lions to play, and leopards to hunt, surely preachers can be trained to preach."[6] Congregations can also be trained to listen!

Specifically, who could benefit from this book?
- Seasoned pastors who need encouragement to "stay the course";
- Mature Christians who love to study all aspects of the ministry of Christ Jesus;

- Seminary professors who introduce their preaching classes with a philosophy of ministry that mirrors Christ's preaching;
- Bible study leaders;
- Evangelists desiring to see how Christ interacted with people;
- Search committees who need to hire pastors after Jesus' own heart;
- New pastors fresh out of seminary;
- Ladies involved in Titus 2 discipleship training;
- Congregations who need to appreciate God-driven preaching;
- Laypeople who love to pray for their pastor;
- Conservative pastors who find themselves in liberal churches.

I have decided to include the full text when quoting the Bible, because many people see simple references and never open their Bibles to look up what the book is saying about the Book. I am one of these guilty as charged. Also, I have kept a large number of endnotes for those who might use this book to teach others.

My prayer is that all readers of this book will be impelled to preach more like Jesus and to listen to preaching like His. Ecclesiological triage will keep the focus on the top priority for Christians today—the person and work of Jesus, the Son of Man. Preaching like Jesus did will take care of every other ill found in the church.

Additionally, it is wise to focus on the Savior and His preaching. Many have their guard up against those who try to cure the church by "preaching the reformation," "preaching TULIP/Calvinism," or "preaching like Richard Sibbes [or your favorite preacher]." Even the most liberal church will initially accept pastors who have a desire to preach like the Lord Himself.

Let's get started with an examination of the Son of David, Jesus Christ the Preacher. With the Messiah as our object of study and focus, may we have a desire to move past mere empirical knowledge and grow in our love for the greatest preacher who ever lived. It is my prayer that the readers of this book be more impressed with the greatness of Jesus Christ, so that their praise of Him will rise to God the Father. Let's follow the premise of Raymond Bailey, who said, "Christ Himself should be ... our preaching model."[7]

Notes

1 **Walter C. Kaiser, Jr.,** *Toward an Exegetical Theology: Biblical Exegesis for Preaching and Teaching* (Grand Rapids: Baker, 1981), 7.

2 **E.C. Dargan,** quoted in **Albert Richmond Bond,** *The Master Preacher* (New York: American Tract Society, 1910), 11.

3 Ibid. 9.

4 This book will examine the words of Jesus in the Gospels. It is readily admitted that some may argue that the passages used in this book are not exactly equivalent to sermons preached today. I agree. The goal of this book is not to wade through all of the words of Christ, determine if they were public declarations resembling sermonic delivery today, and then analyze them; rather, I want to demonstrate how Jesus actually taught the Word of God and then exhort teachers to follow after their Master in His preaching substance and style.

5 **Thomas Watson,** *The Beatitudes: An Exposition of Matthew 5:1–12*, accessed June 2007 from ebooks.reftogo.com/ebook_excerpt/8f/TheBeatitudes001.html.

6 **Erasmus,** quoted in **John Stott,** *Between Two Worlds: The Art of Preaching in the Twentieth Century* (Grand Rapids: Eerdmans, 1982), 213.

7 **Raymond Bailey,** *Jesus the Preacher* (Nashville: Broadman Press, 1990), 14.

Jesus viewed preaching as preeminent

What attracts people to a local church? Some answers might include tradition, friends, family, fellowship, geographic location, or children's programs. But, from a biblical standpoint, what should draw people to any local church? The preaching of God's Word—that must be at the very center of God's assembled flock. Biblical preaching has hit the skids and has been replaced with the latest popular gruel that is deficient in nutrients because it is ashamed of the words of Jesus and His apostles. People attend worship services with consumer mentalities and the wrong object in mind. They go to please "me," not to worship God. Trying to find a preaching class in some seminaries is more akin to a lesson in a scavenger hunt, while management and administration classes multiply like rabbits in the springtime. The obsolescence of preaching is not happening before us, it has already happened.

Should preaching really be relegated to the bottom of the "worship" totem pole? When discussing worship, the majority of churchgoers immediately think of music. People rarely think of the pastor as the "worship leader" (even though he is). They raise their hands to music with a fast tempo, supposedly "feeling" the Holy Spirit, but when the preaching begins, all the hands go down (I have always wondered why, if raising one's hands in worship signifies submission and extreme exaltation, people don't raise their hands when the pastor exposits the Word).

Even a cursory and brief glance at the Gospels conspicuously demonstrates that Jesus viewed preaching as preeminent. For the Savior, there was nothing greater than preaching. Frankly, Jesus ordained preaching. Jesus put a premium on preaching and anything less, therefore, is actually satanic opposition. For Jesus, preaching was never to "fall on hard times."

We laugh when we hear voices from a past generation talk about preaching. Austin O'Malley said, "Sermons are like pie-crust, the shorter the better," and H.L. Mencken said, "What is the function that a clergyman performs in the world? Answer: He gets his living by assuring idiots that he can save them from an imaginary hell. It's a business almost indistinguishable from that of a seller of snake-oil for rheumatism." The laughs should subside when we realize that things have not changed much in our era. John Stott described the current perception of preaching today by saying, "It is an outmoded form of communication in our postmodern age … Some stress the worldwide revolt against authority and others the cybernetics revolution in which ever more sophisticated electronic media will dispense with sermons as surely as the automobile has replaced the horse-drawn carriage."[1] How often have you heard this sentiment: "Who are *you* to preach to *me*?" Preaching has a negative connotation and is often a synonym for critical, harsh, overbearing speech. Thankfully, a quick review of Christ's life will reveal that Jesus loved preaching. You should love preaching too.

Brief exposition of the Gospel of Mark

Let us examine Jesus in the Gospel of Mark and quickly clear up any modern misrepresentation of preaching by seeing the priority Jesus Himself placed on it. We pick up the account of Jesus in Mark 1:

And He [Jesus] healed many who were ill with various diseases, and cast out many demons; and He was not permitting the demons to speak, because they knew who He was (Mark 1:34).

Jesus was healing many people and casting out demons. He even prevented demons from being His messengers. It was an intense time of work as the multitudes were getting completely and organically healed by Jesus. One can image the busy and hectic schedule He was keeping. Suddenly, surprisingly, and strategically, Mark leads the reader to an interlude, an intermission of sorts. The text reads:

In the early morning, while it was still dark, Jesus got up, left the house and went away to a secluded place, and was praying there. Simon and his companions searched for Him; they found Him, and said to Him, "Everyone is looking for You" (Mark 1:35–37).

Why is this textual rest or pause located here? This break from healing and casting out demons serves as a vivid demonstration of the primacy of preaching in the life and ministry of Jesus Christ. Mark's audience needs to remember that there was something more important than healing the body. There were more important issues in life than ridding people of demons. What could be more important? Let's find out. The plot thickens.

Jesus got up "In the early morning, while it was still dark." This forceful time label, containing three Greek adverbs, emphasizes the early nature of the morning hour. The last watch of the night was between 3:00 a.m. and 6:00 a.m., so it is safe to assume that it was still dark outside when Jesus left Simon's house in Capernaum (Mark 1:21, 29). Wanting to be undisturbed, Jesus moved to a lonely, quiet, and out-of-the-way place. This is in direct contrast to the large crowds that He had been dealing with on a regular basis.

Why would Jesus go to this remote, uninhabited place? Earlier in Mark 1, the wilderness and desert was a place for satanic temptation and loneliness. He was going to have a lengthy prayer time with His Father. The Greek word translated "praying" is an imperfect verb designating an ongoing, long prayer time. Certainly this would have been a time of renewal, refreshment, and rejuvenation while Jesus was in the Father's presence. We do not know the exact details of the prayer, but the focus of Mark is on its length. Actually, Mark did not want us to know exactly what Jesus was praying about. We do know it was a protracted time spent with the Father, and it would have likely contained requests for guidance and strength, as well as praise and thanksgiving. The scene flashes back to Simon.

Can you imagine the horror of Simon upon waking up and finding a crowd of people outside his home? R.C.H. Lenski said, "It seems that the crowds of the evening before were already again gathering at Peter's house. Peter and his companions want Jesus to hurry back in order to satisfy the crowds."[2] Everyone is at the house except the most important person—Jesus. I can hear Simon's heart beating two thousand years later. Simon must have had his Adam's apple stuck in his throat as he frantically checked and double-checked each room of the house. Put yourself in his shoes: you have the miracle-working Jesus staying at your house. You arise from your bed anticipating another day of observing the supernatural workings of God incarnate. Simon's first thoughts must have been similar to those of today's children who wake up on Christmas day with anticipation and relish only to find no brightly wrapped presents under the tree. Simon's thoughts were quickly replaced with fear and panic. Jesus had disappeared! There were no notes found, no memos discovered, and no trace of Jesus or His whereabouts. The forehead of Simon was probably getting moister by the minute.

The hunt was officially on. Release the hounds and track down the escapee! Immediately, Simon and company (most likely Andrew, James, and John—Mark 1:29) looked for their healing Master (Mark 1:37). They were trying to stay one step in front of the swelling crowd. The term "look for" in Mark 1:37 does not even approach the intensity of the verb in the original Greek. The word implies to hunt for, track down, or pursue with sweat and single-minded determination. Scholar D. Edmond Hiebert says, "It reflects a recollection of the anxiety of the disciples before they succeeded in locating Jesus."[3] The location of the verb in the sentence lends additional emphasis on the panic felt by the disciples. The intense stress of the situation is highlighted when you consider that this word translated "look" will be later utilized by Mark to depict the intensity of Jesus' enemies seeking to arrest Him and murder the Messiah (Mark 11:18; 12:12; 14:1, 11, 55).

Mark 1:37 says, "They found him, and said to Him, 'Everyone is looking for You.'" Unfortunately, modern translations of this verse cannot portray the weight of emotion in this statement by the disciples. Far from mild or bland, this statement was satiated with an emotional disdain and a "hands-on-hips" type of exasperation. Can't you hear the disciples' tone of voice? After their long search, they effectively said, "More people are at our doorstep expecting a miracle from the Messiah, and without *You* there, what do You expect us to do? Get back to the healing ministry *You* started!" How does Jesus respond? Words cannot fully express the devastation of His reply. The words of Jesus have the effect of a nuclear bomb exploding directly in the faces of His disciples. Read this verse and make sure you place a "selah"[4] after it:

[Jesus] said to them, "Let us go somewhere else to the towns nearby, so that I may preach there also; for that is what I came for" (Mark 1:38).

This is shocking! It must have smacked the men like a cold, wet slap in the face. "Astonishing" is the word that would best describe Jesus' reply. The present tense of "let us go" indicates that Jesus' preaching tour would be a lengthy one. No temporary journey is in the mind of Christ. The crowds and all the people are hunting for Him. The hounds are loosed and are sniffing for their prey. Dramatically, Jesus, with a rebuke, has left all the hubbub in Capernaum for smaller villages, cities, and towns. There will be no monopoly on Jesus and His work. Luke's parallel account describes it this way:

But He said to them, "I must preach the kingdom of God to the other cities also, for I was sent for this purpose" (Luke 4:43).

What is the point? Preaching the good news of God's forgiveness was more important than healing, so Jesus embarked on an extended preaching tour. Preaching the good news of the kingdom took priority over physical healing and the exorcism of humans invaded by demonic hordes. After all, people can be bodily healed and still be eternally doomed. The good news that God saves sinners through His Son is the ultimate and most important message. All the villages needed to hear this message of redemption and liberation. Robert Mounce captures the magnitude and weight of Jesus' "about face" with this analysis:

We are prepared for the prominence of preaching in the ministry of Jesus by His own declaration that it was for this reason that He had come (Mark 1:38). When the ministry of healing threatened to eclipse that of preaching, Jesus drew apart from the clamoring crowd and moved on to the next town. He had come to preach; healing was secondary.[5]

Many years ago I heard Englishman Dick Lucas preaching from this passage in Los Angeles. This section of Mark's account was entitled, "How to ruin your ministry." Lucas said it would take just three easy steps:

1. Get the power to heal all sickness.
2. Get a large crowd of sick people.
3. Turn away and tell them you are going on a preaching trip.[6]

From the human perspective, Jesus had all the wrong priorities.

Miracles have a place, but they are never at the top of the spiritual priorities ladder. If miracles and healings were at the pinnacle of the Lord's ministry, He would have been an excellent candidate to be a P.T. Barnum of the first century, but miracles simply served as a launching pad for preaching. While miracles demonstrated Christ's compassion for people, they also, more importantly, served as a platform for His proclamation. Preaching was preeminent, and miracles and healings were ancillary because spiritual healing was much more vital than physical healing. Healed, whole people will still go to hell unless the preached Word and the saving grace of God interrupt their depravity. Jesus knew preaching was preeminent, and He acted as if this were the case.

An older yet still reliable scholar, Henry Barclay Swete, said, "The Lord's primary mission was to proclaim the Kingdom (i. 14); dispossessing demoniacs and healing the sick were secondary and in a manner accidental features of His work."[7] After John the Baptist's message was muzzled, Jesus came preaching the gospel of the salvation of sinners (Mark 1:14). Nothing was going to stop Jesus. Mark comments, "And He went into their synagogues throughout all Galilee, preaching and casting out the demons" (Mark 1:39). Mark 1 should simplify every agenda in the local church.

Look how the Gospel of Matthew stresses the primacy of Christ's preaching. It is both interesting and unusual. Matthew employed a unique style of writing to show Christ's teaching as climactic and central. He highlighted Jesus' preaching by concluding each of the five preaching/teaching sections with "when Jesus had finished these words" (or something very similar). Matthew's intention was to demonstrate that his narrative sections were often introductory to the main event, which was Jesus' teaching. As a conclusion to the Sermon on the Mount, for example, Matthew wrote, "When Jesus had finished these words, the crowds were amazed at His teaching" (Matthew 7:28).

And just prior to teaching the Twelve, he tells us that "When Jesus had finished giving instructions to His twelve disciples, He departed from there to teach and preach in their cities" (Matthew 11:1). Finally, as a conclusion to the parables, the Bible says, "When Jesus had finished these parables, He departed from there" (Matthew 13:53). The Gospels highlight the preaching ministry of Jesus Christ.

Application for preachers, elders, leaders, and Bible teachers

1. GUARD THE PRIMACY OF PREACHING IN YOUR MINISTRY

If, during Christ's ministry, miracles and healings were forced to the back seat behind the proclamation of the Word, why would anything today ever trump the preaching of the Word? Even though administration, counseling, and a hundred other "profitable" ministries demand attention from the pastor, the preacher, with flint-like determination, must follow the Master's mandate and keep preaching central. Godly men of the past have recognized the common temptations preachers face. R.B. Kuiper elaborated:

Because his duties are manifold, there is great danger that the minister will fail to put first things first; that he will "spread himself thin" ... that he will attempt to do so many things that he does nothing well. Perhaps he will be an administrator rather than a teacher ... He may even turn into the proverbial "jack of all trades," comprising chauffeur, messenger boy and assistant housekeeper. Because he tries to do too much, he may accomplish next to nothing.[8]

Methodology always follows theology, so those who really believe in the strategic nature of preaching will manifest it in their ministries. Conversely, if you allow preaching to play second fiddle to anything or anyone, then you do not actually believe that Jesus considered preaching to be ultimate. Don't get sucked into the worldly blackhole-like advice of church-growth gurus who lament, "Unfortunately, many churches in choosing a pastor place greatest priority on the man's ability to preach. Certainly congregations are entitled to prepared and well-delivered messages. Yet, sermon delivery represents a very small portion of the pastor's total work week. Indications are that the sermon, by itself, is a relatively minor factor in the growth of the church."[9]

Jesus clearly did not use preaching as a springboard to bigger and better things; it was always His top priority on the way to the cross. Detours from preaching God's Word reflect an attitude about preaching that Jesus Himself did not have. Remember, it was Jesus Himself, through the Spirit, who instructed His apostle to write, "Preach the Word" (2 Timothy 4:2ff.). You don't have to be "led" to obey God's clear Word!

Pastor, is preaching at the top of your priority list? If you are a Bible teacher, be resolved in your conviction to preach the Word. You must remember that the purpose of your very existence is to preach God's counsel. In 1900, G. Campbell Morgan pressed the primacy of preaching to a fellow pastor, saying,

Nothing is more needed among preachers today than that we should have the courage to shake ourselves free from the thousand and one trivialities in which we are asked to waste our time and strength, and resolutely return to the apostolic ideal which made necessary the office of the diaconate. [We must resolve that] we will continue stedfastly [sic] in prayer, and in the ministry of the Word.[10]

2. STUDY DILIGENTLY

Because the Bible is God's Word, the preacher must be determined to faithfully exegete and exposit God's Word. John Calvin knew the seriousness of faithful pulpit ministry as he lamented that some preachers deliver sermons "without due care, as though it were some game that we were playing."[11]

Because the most crucial aspect of ministry is the proclamation of the Word of God, give due diligence to study it so that you accurately speak for God. The New Testament unmistakably teaches that the Word of God must be handled accurately and with "due care." The Apostle Paul says to Timothy the pastor, "Be diligent to present yourself approved to God as a workman who does not need to be ashamed, accurately handling the word of truth" (2 Timothy 2:15). Paul wants Timothy, and every pastor and elder after him, to properly interpret and teach the Bible. Paul tells his young apprentice, in the Greek aorist imperative, that he must not spare one iota's worth of effort in the Herculean task of proper hermeneutics, exegesis, and the art of proclamation. The word he uses is σπούδασον, and it means "do one's best, spare no effort, work hard."[12] The *BDAG* lexicon defines it as "to be especially conscientious in discharging an obligation, be zealous/eager, take pains, make every effort, be conscientious."[13] If this word meaning is not emphatic enough, the original language indicates that the word "diligent" is followed by an infinitive. By this, Paul shows the intensity of the command.[14] Paul wants church leaders to faithfully exert themselves in the loftiest of all endeavors—God-honoring Bible teaching.

Timothy must present himself approved to God, and so must you. The use of the second person singular reflexive pronoun σεαυτὸν leaves Timothy no option but to personally give an account of himself to God.[15] He must be the man to execute the imperative. Shame in front of others is one thing, but here Paul states that disobedience will beget shame from God Himself. The word "ashamed" (ἀνεπαίσχυντον) "is passive; it does not merely mean 'ashamed' but 'not forced to be ashamed,' namely by the fatal disapproval of God."[16] Human approval, gain, popularity, and money fade in the light of being shamed before God Himself. Since other viable options are out of the question, Timothy himself "must 'be a workman,' not a quibbler about vain and unprofitable words. The term 'workman' does not point to the needed skill in the performance of his task but rather to the laboriousness involved in its accomplishment. To be an acceptable minister demands strenuous and exhausting toil."[17]

What does this work imply? Timothy must accurately handle the Word of God by interpreting it properly. The literal meaning of ὀρθοτομοῦντα, a present active participle, is "cutting straight."[18] The question is, what does "cutting straight" mean? This word is somewhat controversial, but "recent reference works and commentaries tend to agree that the cutting imagery is less important than the idea of correctness."[19] A detailed word study is quite helpful. Friberg says, "as cutting a straight road through difficult terrain make a straight path; figuratively in the NT, with reference to correctly following and teaching God's message hold to a straight course, teach accurately."[20] Louw-Nida, Thayer, and *BDAG* define the word similarly, based on other appearances of this word in the Bible, specifically in the LXX (Proverbs 3:6; 11:5).[21] *BDAG* elaborates: "It is used w. ὁδούς and plainly means 'cut a path in a straight direction' or 'cut a road across country (that is forested or otherwise difficult to pass through) in a straight direction,' so that the traveler may go directly to his destination."[22] Timothy must teach the truth correctly and not get sidetracked by wordsmiths, debaters, or ungodly talkers. He must teach with clarity and sound doctrine. Does God expect anything less from you?

How can the apostolic traditions and the Word be passed down from generation to generation unless the teaching remains pure and true to the intent of the author? Faulty interpretation leads to the loss of objective truth and ends up yielding a morass of vagueness and subjective understanding. Stott understands the implications, saying, "To 'cut it straight' or 'make it a straight path' is to be accurate on the one hand and plain on the other in our exposition."[23]

This positive command in 2 Timothy 2 also contains an implicit warning against handling the Word wrongly. William Hendricksen describes the man who is obedient to the Lord: "The man who handles the word of the truth properly does not change, pervert, mutilate, or distort it, neither does he use it with a wrong purpose in mind."[24] Accuracy and truthfulness are the goals of the teacher. He is to be in stark opposition to Elymas the magician, of whom Scripture says,

But Elymas the magician (for so his name is translated) was opposing them, seeking to turn the proconsul away from the faith. But Saul, who was also known as Paul, filled with the Holy Spirit, fixed his gaze on him, and said, "You who are full of all deceit and fraud, you son of the devil, you enemy of all righteousness, will you not cease to make crooked the straight ways of the Lord?" (Acts 13:8–10).

You must lay down a trail for others, so that they might follow it. You must teach correctly, and that means you must properly understand and interpret the Bible. Paul "enjoins on every teacher of the Word straightforward exegesis."[25]

Paul goes on to stress the importance of the clear and true teaching charge when he describes Scripture as "the word of truth." George W. Knight III explains it by saying, "The sense of the phrase here is probably best conveyed in the rendering 'message of the truth.' To handle the word correctly is to handle it in accord with its intention and to communicate properly its meaning."[26] What a contrast this truthful message is to any

"Ephesian errorist"![27] All who teach the Bible must interpret it clearly and accurately. Timothy is the example for all who teach, not just pastors. If Timothy's responsibility was so weighty, then he would logically teach others to adequately handle the Word in the same way. Why would Timothy teach or expect anything less from his disciples?

And for those bold enough to pick up the difficult, God-exalting task of sequential expository preaching, let these wise words from Stott roll through your mind as an exhortation:

Expository preaching is a most exacting discipline. Perhaps that is why it is so rare. Only those will undertake it who are prepared to follow the example of the apostles and say, "It is not right that we should give up preaching the Word of God to serve tables ... We will devote ourselves to prayer and to the ministry of the Word" (Acts 6:2,4). The systematic preaching of the Word is impossible without the systematic study of it. It will not be enough to skim through a few verses in daily Bible reading, nor to study a passage only when we have to preach from it. No. We must daily soak ourselves in the Scriptures. We must not just study, as through a microscope, the linguistic minutiae of a few verses, but take our telescope and scan the wide expanses of God's Word, assimilating its grand theme of divine sovereignty in the redemption of mankind. "It is blessed," wrote C.H. Spurgeon, "to eat into the very soul of the Bible until, at last, you come to talk in Scripture language, and your spirit is flavored with the words of the Lord, so that your blood is bibline and the very essence of the Bible flows from you."[28]

Application for laypeople and congregations

1. ENCOURAGE YOUR PASTOR TO KEEP PREACHING AS THE "MAIN EVENT"
This manifests itself in never complaining about the length of the sermon, the biblical content of the sermon, or the depth of content in the sermon. Pray for your pastor's preaching and your church's reception of the sermon.

2. IF YOU FIND YOURSELF ON A PASTORAL SEARCH COMMITTEE, HIRE A PREACHER LIKE JESUS!
Michael Horton illustrates the demise of preaching as he discusses current "want ads" for pastors and how they have changed over time:

One church seeks "a dynamic leader with a passion to facilitate growth." Hence, this person will be given to "relevant, thematic preaching incorporating creative use of drama and contemporary worship." According to another ad, a member of the pastoral staff should possess "gifting in leadership, shepherding, administration, recruiting, team-building, problem solver [sic], large church experience (1,000+)" ... But most of the qualifications had to do with personal abilities that might be sought in any business looking for a combination CEO, coach, and entertainer. From my random sampling of this publication's past several issues, here are the most representative criteria for ministry staff (each word taken directly from the ads).[29]

Heralds should not be primarily known as relational, relevant, dynamic, or team leaders. Paul tells Timothy, and all future pastors, to preach the Word. If Jesus is the example, preaching is nonnegotiable.

3. ASK YOUR PASTOR FOR A BOOK RECOMMENDATION ABOUT WORSHIP

Worship contains giving "worth" to the triune God by singing, certainly, but also by serving, giving, praying, preaching, listening to preaching, baptisms, participation in the Lord's Supper, and Scripture reading. See the Appendix for a list of valuable resource books on worship.

Summary

The most urgent need in the Christian Church today is true preaching and as it is the greatest and most urgent need in the Church, it is obviously the greatest need of the world also.[30]

Notes

1 **John R.W. Stott,** "Biblical Preaching is Expository Preaching" in *Evangelical Roots*, **Kenneth Kantzer,** ed. (Nashville: Thomas Nelson, 1978), 159.

2 **R.C.H. Lenski,** *The Interpretation of St Mark's Gospel* (Minneapolis: Augsburg, 1946), 87.

3 **D. Edmond Hiebert,** *The Gospel of Mark: An Expositional Commentary* (Greenville, SC: Bob Jones University Press, 1994), 56.

4 There is some debate on the meaning of this Hebrew word, but one option is that it indicates a pause for reflection. When describing "selah," Dwight Pentecost used to say, "Stop and let that sink in."

5 **Robert H. Mounce,** *The Essential Nature of New Testament Preaching* (Eugene, OR: Wipf & Stock, 1960), 29.

6 **Dick Lucas,** Sermon on Mark 1 (Ken Jones' Church in Watts, CA, 1996).

7 **Henry Barclay Swete,** *The Gospel According to St Mark* (London: Macmillan and Co., 1908), 27.

8 **R.B. Kuiper,** *The Glorious Body of Christ* (Carlisle, PA: Banner of Truth, 1966), 140–142.

9 **Win Arn,** "How to Find a Pastor Who Fits Your Church," in *The Pastor's Church Growth Handbook* (Pasadena, CA: Church Growth Press, 1979), 12.

10 **G. Campbell Morgan** in **Jill Morgan,** ed., *This Was His Faith: The Expository Letters of G. Campbell Morgan* (Westwood, NJ: Fleming Revell, 1952), 25.

11 **John Calvin,** accessed August 2007 from audio.gracechurch.org/sc/2006notes/Recipe%20for%20Success,%20Hardy.pdf.

12 **Barclay M. Newman,** *A Concise Greek-English Dictionary of the New Testament* [CD-ROM] (United Bible Societies), in *Bible Works* (Norfolk: BibleWorks LLC, 1992–2003), s.v. "σπουδάζω."

13 **Frederick William Danker,** *Greek-English Lexicon of the New Testament and Other Early Christian Literature* (*BDAG*), ed. **Kurt Aland** and **Barbara Aland,** with **Viktor Reichmann,** 3rd ed. [CD-ROM] (Chicago: The University of Chicago Press, 2000), in *Bible Works* (Norfolk: BibleWorks LLC, 1992–2003), s.v. "σπουδάζω."

14 **George Knight** weighs in, saying, "This imperative intensifies the command expressed by the infinitive clause that it governs, σεαυτὸν δόκιμον παραστῆσαι τῷ θεῷ." (**George W. Knight III,** *Commentary on the Pastoral Epistles*, New International Greek Testament Commentary, Grand Rapids: Eerdmans, 1992, 411.)

15 **Knight,** *Commentary on the Pastoral Epistles*, 411.

16 **R.C.H. Lenski,** *The Interpretation of St Paul's Epistles to the Colossians, to the Thessalonians, to Timothy, to Titus and to Philemon* (Minneapolis: Augsburg, 1937, 1946), 798.

17 **D. Edmond Hiebert,** *Second Timothy* (Chicago: Moody, 1958), 67–68.

18 *Thayer's Lexicon* [CD-ROM], in *Bible Works* (Norfolk: BibleWorks LLC, 1992–2003), s.v. "ὀρθοτομέω." This word comes from ὀρθός and τέμνω.

19 **Walter L. Liefeld,** *1 and 2 Timothy, Titus*, The NIV Application Commentary, ed. Terry Muck (Grand Rapids: Zondervan, 1999), 258.

20 *Friberg Lexicon* [CD-ROM], in *Bible Works* (Norfolk: BibleWorks LLC, 1992–2003), s.v. "ὀρθοτομοῦντα."

21 "In all your ways acknowledge Him, and He will make your paths straight" (Proverbs 3:6) and "The righteousness of the blameless will smooth his way, but the wicked will fall by his own wickedness" (Proverbs 11:5).

22 *BDAG*, s.v. "ὀρθοτομοῦντα."

23 John R.W. Stott, *Guard the Gospel* (Downers Grove, IL: InterVarsity Press, 1973), 67.

24 William Hendricksen, *I & II Timothy and Titus* (Grand Rapids: Baker, 1957), 263.

25 E.K. Simpson, *The Pastoral Epistles* (Grand Rapids: Eerdmans, 1954), 4–5.

26 Knight, *Commentary on the Pastoral Epistles*, 412.

27 Hiebert, *Second Timothy*, 68.

28 John R.W. Stott, *The Preacher's Portrait* (London: Billing & Sons, 1961), 30–31.

29 Michael Horton, "Wanted: Ministers who preach not themselves, but Christ," www.modernreformation.org/default.php?page=articledisplay&var1=ArtRead&var2=201&var3=main, accessed July 2007.

30 D. Martyn Lloyd-Jones, *Preaching and Preachers* (Grand Rapids: Zondervan, 1971), 9.

Jesus preached with a high view of Scripture

Confidence in the verity of Scripture is nonnegotiable for the preacher. Any inkling that the Bible has a smidgeon of fiction is lethal to expository preaching. There is an inseparable link between a preacher's view of Scripture and his philosophy of preaching. If the Bible is less than inerrant, infallible, God-breathed, and sufficient, then why would anyone painstakingly preach it? Why bother with grammatical nuances and "the letter of the law" when a bird's-eye view is all that is needed? After all, if fallible man alone wrote the Bible, if it is some human invention, then microanalysis will yield only the frail, fragile, and fallible results of sinful mankind. An attitude that will guarantee a low view of the pulpit ministry is epitomized by Robert Bratcher, one of the translators for the *Good News for Modern Man Bible* paraphrase: "Only willful ignorance or intellectual dishonesty can account for the claim that the Bible is inerrant and infallible. No truth-loving, God-respecting, Christ-honoring believer should be guilty of such heresy."[1] You don't have to listen for long to see, with X-ray-like vision, a behind-the-scenes view of a pastor's bibliology.

A sure antidote to the gravity of an error like Bratcher's (and the others in the chorus of biblical skepticism) is to ponder the ministry of Jesus Christ and observe His full confidence in, and reliance upon, Holy Writ. In other words, the student of Scripture must keep the Savior always in view. While appeals to prophecy, science, and archeology can surely find their place in the arsenal of an honorable bibliology, nothing bolsters an exalted, high view of Scripture than the public ministry of the Son of Man.

The goal of this chapter is to succinctly exhibit the Savior's high view of Scripture. The by-product of sitting at the Lord's feet and observing how He preached will be trust in the Word. This chapter will quickly examine Jesus Christ's perception of the Old Testament (His "Bible" while He was on earth) with the purpose that you will preach expositionally with confidence in the Bible. When a pastor or congregant sees the Word properly, that is, "magnified … above all thy name" (Psalm 138:2, KJV), then he will endeavor to diligently and appropriately preach it with honor, clarity, and accuracy.

My desire is to establish greater buoyancy in the hearts of Bible preachers so that they echo C.H. Spurgeon when he said,

Full assurance of the certainty of what we preach in the name of the Most High God is absolutely necessary to making full proof of our ministry … If the Bible be not believed to be a supernatural book, infallibly teaching the things which make for our eternal salvation, he who, with deliberate falsehood of unbelief, yet uses it as his text-book, and refers to it as his authority, is a trifler with truth, and a mocker of sacred things … If we are ever to see men brought down under the power of the law to a condition of true repentance, if we are ever to see them converted by the Holy Ghost through the gospel of Christ Jesus, if we are ever to see the converted ones sanctified, and marching forth to the Master's battles as an army with banners, we must preach the truth boldly, as we ought to preach it, and we must say of every jot and tittle of it, "Not a doubt of it! Not a doubt of it!"[2]

What Jesus didn't do

The most striking reassurance that the Bible is trustworthy is contained in what Jesus did not do. Far from giving an argument from silence, Jesus, the incarnate God, had ample opportunity to address the inaccuracies in the Old Testament. It had been over 400 years since God had spoken, and the original manuscripts of the Old Testament were long gone. When the Messiah arrived, He could (and would) clear up any errors in the minds of the hearers as well as in the text itself. Jesus would demand the purity of God's Word.

If the Old Testament scrolls had been compromised long before Jesus exclaimed, "Repent," He would have called for a return to the real Word. He would have corrected the problems in the manuscripts or the interpretational problems. The scribes and Pharisees could have been teaching from parchments full of textual corruptions or scribal additions. Frankly, whole books could have been missing from the Old Testament canon, or entire books could have been erroneously added. Jesus could have said, "For too long, the Jewish leaders have thought of the Book of Esther as God-breathed. You are mistaken. This historical book does not even refer to My Father one time. It does not bear the stamp of divine authorship." Instead, Jesus, by His silence and by regularly quoting from the Old Testament, affirmed the legitimacy of the canon that existed in Palestine during His life.

Jesus never quoted an extrabiblical source. Never. Other rabbis of the day quoted a panoply of sources to authenticate their teachings, but Jesus on no account quoted from the apocrypha, psuedopigrapha, or rabbinic traditions (which would one day be formulated into the Mishnah or Talmud). Instead, Jesus liberally and regularly quoted the Old Testament. For example, during His three temptations from Satan, Jesus quoted Deuteronomy all three times. Modern scholar Robert Lightner elucidates Christ's view of the Bible:

It is indeed significant that Christ never even so much as referred to the extra Biblical literature of His day. Many works existed to which He had access and He could have made reference to them but did not do so. He relied solely upon the OT canon of Scripture. Christ always assumed the unquestionable truthfulness and complete trustworthiness of the Holy Scriptures. With divine fervency and frequency He declared its final authority and absolute inviolability. The Savior's attitude toward Scripture, His purposes in using Scripture, His extensive use of Scripture and His methods of interpretation and application, all portray His reverent regard for the Word of God.[3]

Certainly, if true, Jesus would have counseled the scribes about their need to rightly understand the Pentateuch by promoting the "day-age" theory of Genesis 1 or the true human authors of the first five books of Moses, namely "J," "P," "E," or any other supposed person or capital letter. Yet He did none of this. Why? Jesus did not address this topic, because friend and foe believed in Mosaic authorship.

Remember, Jesus never shied away from correcting anyone who had a wrong view of the Scriptures (Matthew 5; Mark 7:1–13; etc.). Yet, amazingly, He never corrected the view in Palestine regarding the canonicity of the Old Testament. It was assumed by Jesus to be authentic even though it was hundreds, and in some parts thousands, of years removed from the original inspiration. Christ's attitude toward the authenticity of the Bible is more amazing because there was not one of the original autographs extant at the time of His ministry.

Jesus did not discount Jonah as a myth or story similar to Hercules, nor did He say it was an allegory or parable of some kind. I once read a fanciful account that said that Jonah is simply an illustration of Israel; the ocean is the Gentiles, the fish is Babylon, and the regurgitation is Israel's return via Ezra. This same account said,

> Surely this is not the record of actual historical events nor was it ever intended as such. It is a sin against the author to treat as literal prose what he intended as poetry ... His story is thus a story with a moral, a parable, a prose poem like the story of the Good Samaritan.[4]

The people in Jesus' day knew only the literal story, yet Jesus was silent. The silence remains deafening.

John MacArthur beautifully pushes the reader to the logical options about Jesus and the validity of the Old Testament, saying,

> When examining the testimony of Jesus about the Scriptures, we have to accept one of three possibilities. The first is that there are no errors in the Old Testament, just as Jesus taught. Second, there are errors, but Jesus didn't know about them. Third, there are errors, and Jesus knew about them, but He covered them up. If the second is true— that the Old Testament contains errors of which Jesus was unaware—then it follows that Jesus was a fallible man, He obviously wasn't God, and we can dismiss the whole thing. If the third alternative is true—that Jesus knew about the errors but covered them up—then He wasn't honest, He wasn't holy, He certainly wasn't God, and again, the entire structure of Christianity washes away like a sand castle at high tide.[5]

J.I. Packer adds, "Jesus Christ, so far from rejecting this principle of biblical authority, accepted and built on it, endorsing it with the greatest emphasis and the full weight of His authority. And the authority to which He laid claim was absolute and unqualified."[6]

What Jesus did do

JESUS' USE OF "IT IS WRITTEN"

Sixty-seven times in the New Testament the English phrase "It is written" occurs. Jesus Himself employed this pronouncement on twenty occasions in the Gospels. The phrase is one word in the Greek, containing urgency, significance, and weight. The Greek word γέγραπται is a verb used to denote the "legal attestation of the law and Old Testament witnesses."[7] This formulaic word introduces the reader to solemn quotations from the Old Testament canon.[8] Jesus frequently cited the Old Testament with this word that served as a launching pad to teach essential truths. It was time to pay attention when Jesus spoke this way.[9]

The tense of "It is written" is a perfect passive. In other words, Jesus is saying that the Old Testament was written and it forever stands written. It has ongoing, eternal relevance and stability. Jesus did not summarize the Old Testament nor did He give the big-picture "gist" of the writers. He quoted exactly from the text, and He did so in such a way that denies the neo-orthodox Barthians breathing room.

For a sampling of the solemn "It is written," look at the seven uses by Jesus in Matthew's Gospel, concentrating on the magnitude and import of each Old Testament quote:

But He answered and said, "It is written, 'Man shall not live on bread alone, but on every word that proceeds out of the mouth of God'" (Matthew 4:4).

Jesus said to him, "On the other hand, it is written, 'You shall not put the LORD your God to the test'" (Matthew 4:7).

Then Jesus said to him, "Go, Satan! For it is written, 'You shall worship the LORD your God, and serve him only'" (Matthew 4:10).

This is the one about whom it is written, "Behold, I send my messenger ahead of you, who will prepare your way before you" (Matthew 11:10).

And He said to them, "It is written, 'My house shall be called a house of prayer'; but you are making it a robbers' den" (Matthew 21:13).

The Son of Man is to go, just as it is written of Him; but woe to that man by whom the Son of Man is betrayed! It would have been good for that man if he had not been born (Matthew 26:24).

Then Jesus said to them, "You will all fall away because of Me this night, for it is written, 'I will strike down the shepherd, and the sheep of the flock shall be scattered'" (Matthew 26:31).

How disingenuous for Jesus to speak with such authority and dogmatism if the Scriptures were anything but 100 percent truth! It would be sheer and shrewd audience manipulation. If He were to appeal to an untrustworthy authority, He would be guilty of egregious personal gain. "It is written" proclaims, with a megaphone-like volume and authority, that the Son of Man believes that Moses and the Prophets are authoritative, sufficient, inerrant, infallible, sure, and clear.

JESUS' USE OF A VERB TENSE

Even the seeming minutia of a proper verb tense rallies the preacher's attitude toward the preciseness of the recorded Word. More than just observing the "big picture" of an Old Testament narrative, Jesus wins a debate with a Hebrew verb tense. The argument was between the Sadducees and Jesus:

On that day some Sadducees (who say there is no resurrection) came to Jesus and questioned Him, asking, "Teacher, Moses said, 'If a man dies having no children, his brother as next of kin shall marry his wife, and raise up children for his brother.' Now there were seven brothers with us; and the first married and died, and having no children left his wife to his brother; so also the second, and the third, down to the seventh. Last of all, the woman died. In the resurrection, therefore, whose wife of the seven will she be? For they all had married her." But Jesus answered and said to them, "You are mistaken, not understanding the Scriptures nor the power of God. For in the resurrection they neither marry nor are given in marriage, but are like angels in heaven" (Matthew 22:23–30).

The influential Sadducees were not to be commended for their inquisitive hearts; rather, Jesus corrects their malicious attempt to force Him to untie the proverbial Gordian knot. They deceitfully give Jesus external respect, calling Him "Teacher," but their true intentions are to discredit the Messiah. The powerful Word is pulled out of its scabbard and is unleashed on the dim-witted Sadducees:

"But regarding the resurrection of the dead, have you not read what was spoken to you by God: 'I am the God of Abraham, and the God of Isaac, and the God of Jacob'? He is not the God of the dead but of the living." When the crowds heard this, they were astonished at His teaching (Matthew 22:31–33).

Confrontations like this are a joy to watch. Jesus declares the error of this aristocratic group by quoting from the part of the Bible in which the Sadducees were especially trained (the Pentateuch). The Sadducees loved the first five books of Moses. They were an Old Testament equivalent to the New Testament's Marcionite Canon. Rebuking them, Jesus asks, "Have you not read …?" because they touted themselves as being knowledgeable. They should have been familiar with the verse Jesus was quoting, namely:

When the LORD saw that he turned aside to look, God called to him from the midst of the bush and said, "Moses, Moses!" And he said, "Here I am." Then He said, "Do not come near here; remove your sandals from your feet, for the place on which you are standing is holy ground." He said also, "I am the God of your father, the God of Abraham, the God of Isaac, and the God of Jacob." Then Moses hid his face, for he was afraid to look at God (Exodus 3:4–6).

Moses is being addressed by God hundreds of years after Abraham, Isaac, and Jacob had been "gathered to their fathers." God is the current, eternal God to these patriarchs because these men are still alive (and so is God). Abraham and his seed are immortal, and they have been resurrected. John MacArthur describes the scene:

Jesus' excellent exegetical argument is based on the emphatic present tense of the *I am* used in that passage from the Pentateuch. After *Abraham* and *Isaac* and *Jacob* were long dead, the Lord was still their *God* every bit as much as when they were alive—in fact, in many ways even more so, because they had become perfectly sinless and their souls were experiencing the fellowship of His eternal presence.[10]

Notice that Jesus does not simply say, "I am the God of Abraham, Isaac, and Jacob." Rather, he communicates the intimacy of God with each of the patriarchs with the repetition of "the God of …": "*the God of* Abraham, *the God of* Isaac, and *the God of* Jacob." God was still their personal God long after they had died. Yet these men must be alive because God is the God of the living.

Luke lends added information demonstrating Jesus' claim and showing that Moses taught the resurrection:

"But that the dead are raised, even Moses showed, in the passage about the burning bush, where he calls the Lord the God of Abraham, and the God of Isaac, and the God of Jacob. Now He is not the God of the dead but of the living; for all live to Him." Some of the scribes answered and said, "Teacher, You have spoken well." For they did not have courage to question Him any longer about anything (Luke 20:37–40).

The people were getting used to being amazed at Christ's teaching. Tragically, with vaccine-like effect, each bold assertion of truth served as "truth inoculation." The recalcitrant hearts of these false teachers did not repent, they recoiled. These scribal cowards tried to save face as they scurried to their lairs of hypocrisy.

JESUS' USE OF "UNBELIEVABLE" OR SUPERNATURAL PASSAGES

Jesus corroborated the historicity and validity of the Old Testament by freely quoting passages about historical people and events. He was immersed in Moses and the Prophets to such a degree that F.B. Meyer proclaimed, "It has been truly said that no disciples of Browning or Tennyson, Milton or Shakespeare, Goethe or Dante, Virgil or Homer, were ever so saturated with their master's thoughts or so steeped in their spirit as Jesus was with Scripture."[11]

Confirmation of the most supernatural sections of the Old Testament has confounded liberal theologians for decades. It is as if the Holy Spirit impelled Jesus to use these verses for two purposes. The first purpose would be the immediate, in-context aim for the situation in which Jesus found Himself. The second would be to give all readers of the Bible confidence in the Old Testament because Jesus quoted from its most humanly unbelievable and supernatural portions.

A quick tour of the Gospels reports Jesus finding these ten people or events historical and real:

1. THE CREATION OF ADAM AND EVE

And He answered and said, "Have you not read that He who created them from the beginning made them male and female, and said, 'For this cause a man shall leave his father and mother and be joined to his wife, and the two shall become one flesh?'" (Matthew 19:4–5).

2. DANIEL

Therefore when you see the abomination of desolation which was spoken of through Daniel the prophet, standing in the holy place (let the reader understand), then those who are in Judea must flee to the mountains. Whoever is on the housetop must not go down to get the things out that are in his house. Whoever is in the field must not turn back to get his cloak (Matthew 24:15–18).

3. CAIN AND ABEL

... from the blood of Abel [found in Genesis] to the blood of Zechariah [found in 2 Chronicles], who was killed between the altar and the house of God; yes, I tell you, it shall be charged against this generation (Luke 11:51).

4. NOAH

For just like the lightning, when it flashes out of one part of the sky, shines to the other part of the sky, so will the Son of Man be in His day. But first He must suffer many things and be rejected by this generation. And just as it happened in the days of Noah, so it will be also in the days of the Son of Man: they were eating, they were drinking, they were marrying, they were being given in marriage, until the day that Noah entered the ark, and the flood came and destroyed them all (Luke 17:24–27).

5. MOSES AND THE BURNING BUSH

But regarding the fact that the dead rise again, have you not read in the book of Moses, in the passage about the burning bush, how God spoke to him, saying, "I am the God of Abraham, and the God of Isaac, and the God of Jacob?" (Mark 12:26).

6. LOT AND HIS WIFE

It was the same as happened in the days of Lot: they were eating, they were drinking, they were buying, they were selling, they were planting, they were building; but on the day that Lot went out from Sodom it rained fire and brimstone from heaven and destroyed them all. It will be just the same on the day that the Son of Man is revealed. On that day, the one who is on the housetop and whose goods are in the house must not go down to take them out; and likewise the one who is in the field must not turn back. Remember Lot's wife (Luke 17:28–32).

7. MOSES LIFTING UP THE SERVANT

As Moses lifted up the serpent in the wilderness, even so must the Son of Man be lifted up; so that whoever believes will in Him have eternal life (John 3:14–15).

8. MANNA FROM HEAVEN

"Our fathers ate the manna in the wilderness; as it is written, 'He gave them bread out of heaven to eat.'" Jesus then said to them, "Truly, truly, I say to you, it is not Moses who has given you the bread out of heaven, but it is My Father who gives you the true bread out of heaven. For the bread of God is that which comes down out of heaven, and gives life to the world" (John 6:31–33).

9. JONAH

But He answered and said to them, "An evil and adulterous generation craves for a sign; and yet no sign will be given to it but the sign of Jonah the prophet; for just as Jonah was three days and three nights in the belly of the sea monster, so will the Son of Man be three days and three nights in the heart of the earth" (Matthew 12:39–40).

10. SODOM AND GOMORRAH

... but on the day that Lot went out from Sodom it rained fire and brimstone from heaven and destroyed them all (Luke 17:29).

Truly I say to you, it will be more tolerable for the land of Sodom and Gomorrah in the day of judgment than for that city (Matthew 10:15).

Jesus confirmed the authority of the Old Testament record. No portion of the Old Testament was a "red-letter" Bible to Him. He did not see the Old Testament as containing the Bible or as being written only by men. Jesus affirmed and confirmed the veracity of the Old Testament.

JESUS' WORDS IN MATTHEW 5:18

Despite the difficulties in interpreting Matthew 5:17–20, one fact remains: Jesus has a high view of the Old Testament. Jesus said in the Sermon on the Mount,

For truly I say to you, until heaven and earth pass away, not the smallest letter or stroke shall pass from the Law until all is accomplished (Matthew 5:18).

With solemn importance ("truly," or "amen"), the Son of God declares the Old Testament Word to have eternal significance. The Bible will outlast all of God's creation ("heaven and earth"). Translating Hebrew words, Christ utilized the vernacular to describe the minutest components of the Hebrew letters, calling them "the smallest letter or stroke," more commonly translated as "one jot or one tittle."[12] To be more precise, the Hebrew *yod* (jot) is the smallest stroke for the Hebrew writer. It is smaller than the smallest letter. Bengel says that there are 66,420 *yods* in the Hebrew Scriptures.[13] What would be the tragedy of losing just one of these 66,420? The calculator on my personal computer gave me an error notice when I tried to divide 1 by 66,420 so that I could figure out the very small percentage of losing just 1 *yod*.

Yes, the least important part of the Old Testament will not pass away until all is accomplished. Think about it: In what portions of the Old Testament Scriptures do the *yods* appear? They occur regularly from Genesis to Malachi (or 2 Chronicles, if you close the Old Testament canon as the Hebrews did). In Luke Jesus proclaimed, "But it is easier for heaven and earth to pass away than for one stroke of a letter of the Law to fail" (Luke 16:17). Not only that, but the "tittle" is "from the Latin *titulus* which came to mean the stroke above an abbreviated word, then any small mark."[14] This small, horn-shaped hook, used to distinguish Hebrew letters, was valuable, part of the canon, and used by Jesus to affirm the validity of the Old Testament.[15] Matthew 5:18 is invaluable in reminding pastors of the credibility of the Old Testament.

JESUS' WORDS IN LUKE 24

The Old Testament set the course for Christ's life. This would be apparent without Luke 24, but it is magnified by this closing chapter in Luke's Gospel.

Now He said to them, "These are My words which I spoke to you while I was still with you, that all things which are written about Me in the Law of Moses and the Prophets and the Psalms must be fulfilled." Then He opened their minds to understand the Scriptures, and He said to them, "Thus it is written, that the Christ would suffer and rise again from the dead the third day, and that repentance for forgiveness of sins would be proclaimed in His name to all the nations, beginning from Jerusalem" (Luke 24:44–47).

The Old Testament's reliability manifests itself by the fulfillment of Messianic prophecies. The Hebrew Scriptures predicted the conception, life, work, death, and resurrection of Jesus Christ. Jesus taught His disciples these truths while He was on earth and stressed each segment of the Scriptures (Law, Prophets, and Psalms). Speaking of this prophetic accomplishment, Meyer rightly opined, "He was guided in the jots and tittles of His life and ministry by His Father's will as it was expressed through Scripture and mapped out there."[16]

Application for preachers, elders, leaders, and Bible teachers

1. WORSHIP GOD BY HAVING A HIGH VIEW OF HIS WORD

John Calvin's reported comments provide the modern pastor with an action item: "We owe to Scripture the same reverence which we owe to God."[17] David describes this devotion in Psalm 119:48, singing, "And I shall lift up my hands to Your commandments, which I love; and I will meditate on Your statutes." Since God's Word is so exalted, preach it with reverence by viewing it as Christ did.

2. SAY REPEATEDLY FROM THE PULPIT, "IT IS WRITTEN," "THE BIBLE SAYS," AND "THUS SAITH THE LORD" (and back up what you say with sequential exposition)

3. REGULARLY TEACH YOUR CONGREGATION (OR THOSE YOU TEACH) CHRIST'S WORSHIPFUL ATTITUDE TOWARD THE BIBLE

4. SINCE JESUS GAVE HIS DIVINE STAMP OF APPROVAL TO THE FULL CORPUS OF SCRIPTURE, TEACH FROM "ABEL TO ZECHARIAH" (GENESIS TO 2 CHRONICLES) IN THE OLD TESTAMENT AND FROM MATTHEW TO REVELATION IN THE NEW TESTAMENT

Meyer declared, "Our Lord's profound reverence and love for the Scripture should make every minister desire that during his pastorate he should succeed in leading his people to a well-balanced and intimate acquaintance with the entire range of the Word of God, that they may be thoroughly furnished unto all good works."[18]

5. CREATE A SYSTEMATIC APPROACH TO TEACH EVERY BOOK OF THE BIBLE

I generally teach from the New Testament in the morning service and from the Old Testament in the evenings. Are you willing to teach every verse of the Song of Solomon? The best way to accomplish a goal like this is to plan out your preaching schedule (it is okay if your plan changes over time; everything is "Lord willing").

6. BE RESOLVED TO TEACH THE SCRIPTURES STRESSING THE INTENT OF THE AUTHOR

"Authorial intent" asks the question, "What did God, through the human author, intend the original readers to understand about this passage?" The passage's meaning should be the central thrust of the sermon. Scripture should determine its own meaning. Walter Liefeld puts it this way: "We reverently ask God, 'Why did you put this here?' I am not only asking what the teaching is but why it is given here."[19] Our sermons should never homiletically manipulate the text for oratorical effect. This distortion would not coincide with the high view that Jesus had of Holy Writ.

Looking through the eyes of the reader, to see how he or she sees things, feels, etc., is valid when it comes to applying the text from the pulpit, but reader-response theories are not valid in the hermeneutical or exegetical process. The pastor's job is to determine what God the Holy Spirit said through His chosen and inspired authors and then to proclaim it. The text is not a launching point for man's wisdom, an "encounter," or a display of the pastor's eloquence. It is not to be used to create an "aha" moment in the mind of the hearer. Instead, it is a sacred declaration of God's Word that stands over men and judges them. It should never be used to facilitate an opportunity to parade the wisdom of men. This is the tragic, but logical, stepping-stone to a sermon that is concerned with telling the people something different from that which God intended when He wrote it. I was appalled by David Buttrick when he, after 457 pages of his book intended to teach people to preach, said, "So, let us be willing to say baldly that it is possible to preach the Word of God without so much as mentioning scripture … If scripture should become the *law* of preaching, then preaching will no longer be the Word of God."[20] No wonder he does not even capitalize the "s" of "scripture"! I cannot think of anything that fires me up more than this kind of blatant disregard for the Word, because it motivates me to preach God's Holy Scriptures, even if no one else will, with a view toward its inerrancy, infallibility, authority, and sufficiency. What about you?

7. BE THANKFUL FOR RECEIVING THE PRIVILEGE
OF TEACHING AN OMNI-RELEVANT BIBLE

The eternal, unchanging Word is always "in". Jesus' handling of the Old Testament pulverizes all challengers, such as Robert Green Ingersoll, who stridently commented, "If a man would follow, today, the teachings of the Old Testament, he would be a criminal. If he would follow the teachings of the New, he would be insane."[21]

8. DO NOT TEACH ANYTHING WITH LESS AUTHORITY
OR SUFFICIENCY THAN THE BIBLE

Be an expert in the Bible and leave philosophy, psychology, politics, and business analysis to others! Martin Luther understood God's sufficiency: "I have covenanted with my Lord that he should not send me visions or dreams or even angels. I am content with this gift of the Scriptures, which teaches and supplies all that is necessary, both for this life and that which is to come."[22]

9. IF YOU STRUGGLE WITH THE AUTHENTICITY OF THE BIBLE, THE PRUDENT COURSE OF ACTION IS TO ABANDON (POSTPONE) PREACHING UNTIL YOU ARE SURE OF THE RELIABILITY OF THE WORD[23]

Application for laypeople and congregations

1. DO NOT GET BOGGED DOWN IN DEFENDING THE BIBLE TO UNBELIEVERS
Keep Christ's view in mind and preach forgiveness to your unsaved friends. Put all your energy into the discussion about sin, God's attributes, and the substitutionary death of Christ.

2. READ NORMAN L. GEISLER AND WILLIAM NIX'S
  A GENERAL INTRODUCTION TO THE BIBLE[24]
For a thorough yet understandable overview of issues surrounding the reliability and canonicity of the Bible, read this textbook.

Notes

1 **Robert Bratcher,** "Inerrancy: Clearing Away Confusion," in Christianity Today 25/10 (May 29, 1981), 12.
2 **Charles Haddon Spurgeon,** "Not a Doubt of It!" accessed July 2007 from teampyro.blogspot.com/2007_07_01_archive.html.
3 **Robert P. Lightner,** A Biblical Case for Total Inerrancy: How Jesus Viewed the Old Testament (Grand Rapids: Kregel, 1978), 11.
4 **Julius A. Bewer** in **Hinckley G. Mitchell, John Merlin Powis Smith** and **Julius A. Bewer,** A Critical and Exegetical Commentary on Haggai, Zechariah, Malachi and Jonah (The International Critical Commentary; Edinburgh: T & T Clark, 1912), Section III, 4.
5 **John MacArthur,** Unleashing God's Word in Your Life [CD-ROM] (Nashville: Thomas Nelson, Inc., 2003), 68.
6 **J.I. Packer,** "Fundamentalism" and the Word of God (Grand Rapids: Eerdmans, 1958, 1988), 54.
7 Friberg, s.v. "γράφω."

8 *BDAG*, s.v. "γράφω."

9 Jesus said "It is written" seven times in Matthew, six in Mark, six in Luke, and once in the Gospel of John.

10 John MacArthur, *Matthew 16–23*, MacArthur's New Testament Commentary [CD-ROM] (Chicago: Moody, 1988) in *QuickVerse 7.0* (Hiawatha, IA: Parsons Technology, Inc., 1997).

11 F.B. Meyer, *Expository Preaching: Plans and Methods* (London: Hodder & Stoughton, 1910), 76.

12 James Montgomery Boice, *The Sermon on the Mount: Matthew 5–7* (Grand Rapids: Baker, 2002), 75.

13 Bengel, quoted in **Leon Morris,** *The Gospel According to Matthew*, The Pillar New Testament Commentary, ed. **D.A. Carson** (Grand Rapids: Eerdmans, 1992), 109.

14 A.T. Robertson, *Word Pictures in the Greek New Testament* (Nashville: Broadman Press, 1934) in *Bible Works* [CD-ROM] (Norfolk: BibleWorks LLC, 1992–2003), "Matthew 5:17."

15 John R.W. Stott, *Christian Counter-Culture: The Message of the Sermon on the* Mount, The Bible Speaks Today (Downers Grove: InterVarsity Press), 73.

16 Meyer, *Expository Preaching*, 75.

17 John Calvin, quoted in Steve Lawson, *The Expository Genius of John Calvin* (Lake Mary, FL: Reformation Trust, 2007), 27.

18 Meyer, *Expository Preaching*, 84.

19 Walter Liefeld, *New Testament Exposition* (Grand Rapids: Zondervan, 1984), 97.

20 David G. Buttrick, *Homiletic Moves and Structures* (Philadelphia: Fortress Press, 1987), 458.

21 Robert G. Ingersoll, third interview on Rev. Talmadge, 1882, accessed from www.atheismquotes.com/quotelist.php?subject=7.

22 Attributed to Martin Luther.

23 Start with the book edited by **Norman L. Geisler,** *Inerracy* (Grand Rapids: Zondervan, 1980), and **R. Laird Harris,** *Inspiration and Canonicity of the Scriptures* (Greenville, SC: A Press, 1995).

24 Norman L. Geisler and **William Nix,** *A General Introduction to the Bible* (Chicago: Moody Press, 1968).

Jesus preached Christ, and Him crucified

J esus of Nazareth preached Christ, and Him crucified. It sounds strange but it is true, albeit anachronistic. The central aim and object of the Messiah's preaching was Himself, the Eternal Son. Many books today rightly discuss the obligation of preaching Jesus Christ, but few investigate how the Son of Man preached, specifically, how He preached about Himself.

Paul said, "For we do not preach ourselves but Christ Jesus as Lord" (2 Corinthians 4:5). But Paul's Lord, Jesus, did the very opposite of what Paul stated. The Son of Man preached Himself, specifically, Christ Jesus as Lord! Jesus regularly asserted Himself with a holy boldness: "And I, if I am lifted up from the earth, will draw all men to Myself" (John 12:32). Jesus was often the object of His preaching. Jesus proclaimed Himself "in season and out of season."

This chapter seeks to demonstrate what most take for granted. The thought is so simple that it has remained submerged in the depths of obviousness. To preach Christ and Him crucified is to preach as Jesus Himself preached. The Westminster Catechism's first question is, "What is the chief end of man?" The Catechism's answer is, "Man's chief end is to glorify God, and enjoy Him forever." It has been positively altered by modern teachers who now ask, "What is the chief end of God?" The answer is astounding: "God's chief end is to glorify Himself and enjoy Himself forever." Jesus glorified God as He preached His own person and work. Modern homiletics books rarely include this fact, but several older preaching books held this opinion. Consider the following quotes showing how they saw Jesus as the theme of His own messages:

The Preacher (Jesus) had a unique relation to His message. His preaching was Christo-centric. He was its centre and power. He claimed chief place for honor and worship …

Without Jesus the Person the preaching of Jesus would have been valueless. In Himself must be found the justification for His preaching.[1]

The one feature in Christ's preaching that might seem to offer an aspect of originality, consists in this, that the ultimate subject and object of his preaching was himself. No other teacher is in this regard comparable to Jesus ... 'One is your Master, even Christ;' 'Come unto me, all ye that labor and are heavy laden and I will give you rest;' 'Ye will not come to me that ye might have life;' 'I am the way, and the truth, and the life;' 'No man cometh unto the Father, but by me.' Extraordinary, unparalleled claims; still, it was only in the article of his thus identifying himself with the promised Messiah, that Jesus propounded in them anything to be called new.[2]

His supreme object lesson, of course, was himself.[3]

While no one else should ever preach himself, Jesus did. What an odd but great thought. If anyone else in the universe promoted and preached himself, he would be thought of as the world's greatest egomaniac, yet Jesus, being God incarnate, rightfully declared the truth about Himself and His mission. It is true that the Son frequently promoted His Father's glory, yet He simultaneously gave witness to His own glory.

The Synoptic Gospels are replete with examples of Jesus discussing Himself as the Son of Man, but let us briefly turn our attention to the Gospel of John for a sweeping overview of Jesus' self-centered preaching. John records seven "I am" statements which draw crisp notice to the deity of Jesus of Nazareth. One single "I am" statement is shocking and startling enough, but the seven combined self-attestations of Jesus Christ crystallize the verity that "Christ preached Himself."

Martin Luther called the Gospel of John "the unique, tender, genuine chief Gospel ... Should a tyrant succeed in destroying the Holy Scriptures and only a single copy of the epistle to the Romans and the Gospel according to John escape him, Christianity would be saved."[4] Christianity would be safe because John unmistakably broadcasts Jesus' divinity. All seven "I am" proclamations "have been written so that you may believe that Jesus is the Christ, the Son of God, and that believing you may have life in His name" (John 20:31).

1. Jesus preached Himself as the bread of life

Jesus said to them, "I am the bread of life; he who comes to Me will not hunger, and he who believes in Me will never thirst" (John 6:35).

True believers are told they will not hunger and will never thirst. The Greek word for "not" in 6:35 is used because the author desires to make his statement more emphatic and solemn. The word "never," used in the same verse, means "not at any time will this be true." Jesus, as spiritual nourishment Himself, "contains in himself the source of heavenly life [and] supplies celestial nutriment to souls that they may attain to life eternal."[5] Jesus did not say that He had the bread, or that He knew where to get this bread and how to bake it, rather He preached Himself as the bread of life. The Messiah alone can give spiritual satisfaction in a permanent manner. Bread like this will satiate the hunger in the soul of any spiritual beggar.

2. Jesus preached Himself as the Light of the world

Then Jesus again spoke to them, saying, "I am the Light of the world; he who follows Me will not walk in the darkness, but will have the Light of life" (John 8:12).

The "again" in 8:12 points to Jesus speaking additionally at the Feast of Tabernacles.[6] (John 7:2 indicates the setting for Christ's statement: "Now the feast of the Jews, the Feast of Booths, was near.") The celebration of the feast expanded over the years because of human traditions. Oversized menorahs (scholars debate whether there were three or four menorahs), or Jewish candelabra, were set ablaze in the Court of the Women. The great lights symbolized the "pillar of light" in the wilderness and also illuminated the court as the dancing, singing, and rejoicing continued nightly. These all served to highlight the "I am the Light of the world" declaration. Christ's self-avowal in this very public place would not be missed by the listeners. It was Intentional with a capital "I." Picture Jesus preaching with the menorahs blazing behind Him!

When Jesus said, "He who follows Me will not walk in the darkness, but will have the Light of life," the people must have been stunned. Jesus' words meant, "The Menorah was to be extinguished after the feast, but his light would remain."[7] God, the ultimate source of light, is fully manifest in the Son. Earlier, John wrote, "In Him was life, and the life was the Light of men" (John 1:4). Jesus preached Himself as the Son of God giving light and salvation to His people. Darkness, death, and spiritual groping would be abolished. Belief in Him would yield the pleasure of experiencing God's light.

Jesus was bearing witness to Himself as the God who illuminates (Isaiah 60:19–22; Zechariah 14:5b–7; cf. Revelation 21:23–24), who is light, and who conquers sin and all its darkness. Those following Jesus as if they followed the pillar of cloud by day and the pillar of fire by night would enjoy the promise of walking in the light, but more importantly they would have the promise of having Jesus, the Light. The Pharisees railed against this. They knew Jesus "preached Himself" as they used the language of self-attestation in John 8:13: "So the Pharisees said to Him, 'You are testifying about Yourself; Your testimony is not true.'"

3. Jesus preached Himself as the door of the sheep

So Jesus said to them again, "Truly, truly, I say to you, I am the door of the sheep" (John 10:7).

Correct understanding of this passage is hindered if you think in a twenty-first century, Western way. Near Eastern shepherds regularly examined each sheep as the flock entered the sheep pen for the night. Jesus, the door, proclaims Himself as the only One who decides who penetrates His sheep pen. Jesus calls false messiahs "thieves and robbers" (John 10:8), but He declares Himself as follows: "I am the door; if anyone enters through Me, he will be saved, and will go in and out and find pasture" (John 10:9).

4. Jesus preached Himself as the good shepherd

Jesus makes explicit that which is implicit in "I am" statement 3:

I am the good shepherd; the good shepherd lays down His life for the sheep (John 10:11).

Jesus as shepherd guides and protects His followers. The Messiah grants an abundant, rich life stemming from His sacrifice for the sheep He loves.

Jesus preaches that He is the One who will willingly substitute Himself for sinners. Three times in the section Jesus directly says that He will lay down His life on behalf of, or for the sake of, others (10:11, 15, 17). He forfeits His own life because He is "good," which can also be translated "right, proper, fitting, honorable, or noble." The Son of God preaches Himself as the noble substitutionary sacrifice, which is a far cry from hirelings.

5. Jesus preached Himself as the resurrection and the life[8]

The scene is familiar:

Martha then said to Jesus, "Lord, if You had been here, my brother would not have died. Even now I know that whatever You ask of God, God will give You." Jesus said to her, "Your brother will rise again." Martha said to Him, "I know that he will rise again in the resurrection on the last day." Jesus said to her, "I am the resurrection and the life; he who believes in Me will live even if he dies, and everyone who lives and believes in Me will never die. Do you believe this?" She said to Him, "Yes, Lord; I have believed that You are the Christ, the Son of God, even He who comes into the world" (John 11:21–27).

Martha was well versed in Old Testament theology. She was assured that God would stay true to His promises and resurrect saints on the last day. Jesus lovingly explained to her that, in fact, she was now in the "last days," the days of the Messiah Himself. He preached that He Himself is "the resurrection" and "the life." Both nouns have definite articles in English and in the original Greek,[9] signifying that Jesus personally grants the resurrection and eternal life. He wanted Martha to know that the significance is on the Person, not on the event itself, so He preached Himself to her. Martha did not say, "Quit talking about yourself," or "Self-exalting speech is criticized in the Proverbs." No; she, with Peter-like confession, called Jesus "the Christ."

6. Jesus preached Himself as the way, the truth, and the life

Thomas said to Him, "Lord, we do not know where You are going, how do we know the way?" Jesus said to him, "I am the way, and the truth, and the life; no one comes to the Father but through Me" (John 14:5–6).

This time, Jesus' auto-proclamation is a response to Thomas. Christ tells Thomas He alone has access to the Father. Pluralistic syncretism shudders at this bold declaration. Jesus is not saying that He can teach them the way to the Father (as if the problem were knowledge), but that He Himself is the way to God, the truth of God, and the life of God. Jesus is the way because He is the incarnation of God's revelation and the only One who bestows eternal life.

7. Jesus preached Himself as the true vine

I am the true vine, and My Father is the vinedresser (John 15:1).

Christ Jesus announced that He was the source of spiritual vitality. The *Friberg Lexicon* describes "vine" as "metaphorically, of Christ as sustaining and spiritually nurturing his disciples (JN 15.1); by metonymy, to indicate the produce that a plant produces (RV 14.19)."[10] Jesus grants strength and life to His people as a grapevine would yield sustenance to its grapes.

Summary

Much more could be produced from the corpus of Scripture, but these seven statements of Christ leave no room to doubt that Jesus determined to preach Himself, and Him crucified.

Application for preachers, elders, leaders, and Bible teachers

1. BE RESOLVED TO PREACH JESUS CHRIST EVERY SINGLE TIME YOU STEP INTO THE SACRED DESK

For I determined to know nothing among you except Jesus Christ, and Him crucified (1 Corinthians 2:2).

Paul's deliberate resolve reflects the model of his Master and Lord. With constancy and purpose, the apostle preached the person and work of the Messiah. Make it your business, your job, or occupation to exalt Jesus. Forget the four Ps of Madison Avenue's marketing (product, place, price, and promotion) and "lift high the cross" in the garb of plain truth. The words of 1 Corinthians 2:2 could alternatively be translated, "I determined to know nothing among you except Jesus Christ, *even* Him crucified." The worldly Corinthians might not like a crucified Messiah, but Paul consciously decided to jettison all modern rhetorical devices. Paul gave the listeners what they needed, not that for which they were lusting.

The alternative is deadly. Consider the words of several theologians:

> The disappearance of which I am speaking is not the same as the abduction of a child who is happily playing at home one minute and then is no longer to be found the next. No one has abducted theology in this sense. The disappearance is closer to what happens in homes where the children are ignored and, to all intents and purposes, abandoned. They remain in the home, but they have no place in the family. So it is with theology in the Church. It remains on the edges of evangelical life, but it has been dislodged from its center (David Wells).[11]

> A brilliant young preacher went to his first church, full of pride, learning, and forensic ability. His congregation had a certain pride too, in this newly acquired product of the theological seminary, with 2 degrees after his name and many ohs! and ahs! after his breathless perorations. But they missed something. One day when the young man entered his pulpit, crammed with reason and rhetoric, he saw a note pinned on his pulpit bearing the legend, "Sir, we would see Jesus" (attributed to John Piper).

> A sermon without Christ is no sermon (T. Hoekstra).[12]

> Christ is the only King of your studies, but homiletics is the queen (Robert G. Rayburn).[13]

> Is it possible to preach a Christian sermon without mentioning Jesus? (Graeme Goldsworthy).[14]

> Superficial views of the work of Christ produce superficial Christian lives (D. Martyn Lloyd-Jones).[15]

2. PREACH CHRIST TO KEEP THE FOCUS OF THE SERMON OFF YOU

The pastor who makes himself the star of every sermon is a pitiful man. He should be the mouthpiece of the Lord God, not the focal point of the message. James Denney is reported to have said, "You cannot at the same time give the impression that you are a great preacher and that Jesus Christ is a great Savior." Be sure to concentrate on the systematic exposition of Jesus and His Word, and remain thankful that God would use a sinner like you. Wayne McDill knows God's condescension in using weak preaching and preachers: "I am amazed that God has chosen to make Himself known through preaching. If you were God, would you trust the kingdom into the hands of the preachers you know?"[16] Preach Christ, because you are not strong enough to carry the weight of the congregation on your back.

Since the goal of all preaching is the glorification of God by the exaltation of His Son through the Spirit-inspired Word, follow this advice: "Good expository preaching does not impress the congregation; it feeds them."[17]

3. PREACH CHRIST TO AVOID MORALISTIC PREACHING

The growing tendency in evangelicalism has been to slip into the error of moralistic, "how to," seminar-type sermons. Preachers essentially deliver sermons that call Christians to be more like Christ without showing them Christ and His resources of grace. Instead, Christians need to be reminded that they are "in Christ," and then they should be called to become more of who they are by the power of the Spirit working in them.

Michael Fabarez diagnoses the problem, saying, "People-centered sermons are often symptomatic of people-centered ministries. People-centered ministries are those that have adopted the belief and/or practice of making people and their benefit the ultimate goal of their ministries."[18] Preachers following Christ's model will avoid this rut and thus evade Donald Barnhouse's frightening scenario: "If Satan really were to take over a city, the following would happen: the bars would close, no alcohol would be sold; there would be happy marriages and well behaved children, no crime and everyone would be in churches on Sunday where Christ IS NOT PREACHED."[19]

Weekly sermons about happy marriages, contentment in relationships, self-esteem boosters, how to get along at family gatherings, and financial prosperity all reek of the scent of man-centeredness. A preaching philosophy focused on men will invariably take any passage and spin it to conform to the congregation's sinful bent. Such preachers think nothing of dislocating passages from their context. Michael Horton correctly bemoans such vapidity:

Whenever the story of David and Goliath is used to motivate you to think about the "Goliaths" in your life and the "Seven Stones of Victory" used to defeat them, you have been the victim of moralistic preaching. The same is true whenever the primary intention of the sermon is to give you a Bible hero to emulate or a villain to teach a lesson, like "crime doesn't pay," or, "sin doesn't really make you happy." Reading or hearing the Bible in this way turns the Scriptures into a sort of Aesop's Fables or Grimm's Fairy Tales, where the story exists for the purpose of teaching a lesson to the wise and the story ends with, "and they lived happily ever after."[20]

Sermons are not "Life Perspectives" designed to get the congregation through another week, to be accompanied by a five-point checklist conveniently detachable by the perforations in the bulletin.[21] Congregants have been missing the grandeur, glory, and transcendent greatness of God all week long and are starving for a Word from and about their Savior and Lord, Jesus Christ.

Choose a Gospel and then begin to preach through it verse by verse. You will weekly show people the greatness and glory of Jesus Christ. If I had to do it all over again, I would have picked Matthew instead of James as my first Sunday book to preach (I picked James to challenge the church). If you are a new pastor, choose a Gospel to preach through expositionally and show off Jesus Christ. "Feed My sheep!"

4. PREACH CHRIST TO CIRCUMVENT BIBLE-CHARACTER PREACHING

Evangelical pastors comprehend the fact that the triune God is the real hero of the Old Testament, but that belief is not always fleshed out in methodology. Too many pastors preach anthropocentrically, concentrating on one of the more than 2,900 different Bible characters. The focus needs to be on God and not on humans. The great news is that the Lord employs sinful humans for His greater good, but He is always the One to be applauded and worshiped. It is His fame that should be increased. Sidney Greidanus wisely concludes:

In preparing the sermon, one would do well to remember that people are edified neither by an oratorical performance nor by information about certain Bible characters; rather, people are built up as they hear God's word about the covenant God who makes history with people, now as well as then.[22]

"Dare to be a Daniel" sermons may motivate, but the pastor's primary intention must be to highlight the triune God of Daniel.[23] When David kills Goliath, the text offers the pastor ample opportunity to homiletically magnify the LORD of hosts (1 Samuel 17:45–47) who protects the Davidic line, who wins battles for His people, and who will keep His promise to Abraham. Similarly, the Book of Ruth should spotlight God, not Ruth, Naomi, or any other character. Of Ruth, Daniel Block said, "The author's aim is to explain how, in the providence of God, the divinely chosen King David could emerge from the dark period of the judges."[24] David's line will beget the Messiah, and God will never go back on His promises to Israel and Judah.

5. PREACH CHRIST FROM THE OLD TESTAMENT

Some quotes never leave you. For example, Greidanus memorably says, "One ought not to overlook the fact that a Christian sermon on an Old Testament passage ought to be different from a sermon preached by a Jewish rabbi."[25] Did you know that you could preach the Old Testament with perfect exegesis, correct context, beautiful parsing of the Hebrew verbs, yet fall flat on your face if you don't preach Jesus Christ? On the other hand, I do not believe that Jesus Christ can be found in every verse in the sense of extreme typology à la A.W. Pink or Martin Luther.

The difficulty of avoiding these two extremes must not paralyze the expositor because he is responsible to teach all of God's Word. Jesus preached Himself using the Old Testament and even said in John 5:39–40, 46,

You search the Scriptures because you think that in them you have eternal life; it is these that testify about Me; and you are unwilling to come to Me so that you may have life ... For if you believed Moses, you would believe Me, for he wrote about Me.

Bond knows that preachers need exhortation to accomplish this difficult task, declaring, "Omit Christ as the definite and sufficient end, and these sacred books [the Old Testament] would contain but the story of national failure and unrealized religious aspirations."[26]

Maybe the best advice is from Sinclair Ferguson. Far from preachers naturally understanding how to preach Christ from the Old Testament, they must study and learn it. Ferguson taught,

In particular we must learn to preach Christ from the Old Testament without falling into the old traps of an artificial exegesis. But how do we legitimately preach the text of the Old Testament as those who stand on this side of Pentecost? … Yet we must also preach the Scriptures without denuding them of the genuine historical events they record and the reality of the personal experiences they describe or to which they were originally addressed. How, then, do we preach Christ, and him crucified without leapfrogging over these historical realities as though the Old Testament Scriptures had no real significance for their own historical context?[27]

Purchase a book on the merits or demerits of "redemptive-historical preaching." Dust off your old seminary books and study the hermeneutical principles of valid typology.

6. PREACH JESUS AS THE REMEDY FOR FALLEN MAN'S PROBLEM

When sinners are found in the Bible, the Savior of these sinners can be easily and naturally preached (even if the passage is not about Jesus). Bryan Chapell uses a "fallen condition focus" to make a connection between sinful people in the Bible and modern audiences. He defines the fallen condition focus as "the mutual human condition that contemporary believers share with those to or for whom the text was written that requires the grace of the passage."[28]

Application for laypeople and congregations

1. ATTEND CORPORATE WORSHIP WITH EXPECTATIONS TO HEAR ABOUT JESUS CHRIST, NOT YOUR FELT, PERCEIVED, OR "REAL" NEEDS

2. DO NOT DESIRE PREACHING THAT REVOLVES GOD AROUND YOU

Ask the Lord to give you a heart for God-centered Bible preaching. If the passage does not seem to apply to you, rejoice in the faithfulness of your pastor and be glad that the sermon is ministering to others.

3. DO NOT GAUGE THE SUCCESS OF YOUR CHURCH BY EXTERNALS

The proverbial ABCs of success in postmodern Christianity are assets, buildings, and cash. God measures churches by faithfulness and nothing else (see Revelation 2–3).

Do not worry about numbers if your church preaches Christ Himself. God will bless His Word and bestow the temporal or spiritual blessings as He sovereignly sees fit. Truth proceeding from the pulpit should give you confidence of the Lord's working in your church. On the flip side, David Wells says, "If Christian assumptions are to be allowed to have their place, we cannot assume that success in a cultural market is necessarily an indication of the presence of truth and virtue."[29]

Notes

1 **Albert Richmond Bond,** *The Master Preacher* (New York: American Tract Society, 1910), 93.

2 **William Cleaver Wilkinson,** *Modern Masters of Pulpit Discourse* (New York: Funk & Wagnalls, 1905), 474.

3 **Francis J. Handy,** *Jesus the Preacher* (New York: Abingdon-Cokesbury Press, 1946), 76.

4 **Martin Luther,** quoted in **James Montgomery Boice,** *The Gospel of John, vol. 4: Peace in the Storm (John 13–17)* (Grand Rapids: Baker, 2005), 13.

5 *Thayer's Lexicon,* s.v. "ἄρτος."

6 **Larry Walker** writes, "The feast began on the fifteenth day of Tishri (the seventh month), which was five days after the day of atonement. It lasted for seven days (Lev. 23:36; Deut. 16:13; Ezek. 45:25). On the first day, booths were constructed of fresh branches of trees. Each participant had to collect twigs of myrtle, willow, and palm in the area of Jerusalem for construction of the booths (Neh. 8:13–18). Every Israelite was to live for seven days in these during the festival, in commemoration of when their fathers lived in such booths after their Exodus from Egypt (Lev. 23:40; Neh. 8:15). The dedication of Solomon's Temple took place at the feast (1 Kings 8:2)." *Holman Bible Dictionary*, ed. Trent C. Butler [CD-ROM] in QuickVerse 7.0 (Hiawatha, IA: Parsons Technology, Inc., 1997).

7 **Merrill C. Tenney,** *John,* in vol. 9 of *The Expositor's Bible Commentary,* ed. **Frank E. Gaebelein** and **J.D. Douglas** [CD-ROM] (Grand Rapids: Zondervan, 1981), 92.

8 Some split this confession into two "I am"s, noting the double articles. We will consider it as one for the sake of the discussion.

9 ἡ ἀνάστασις καὶ ἡ ζωή

10 *Friberg Lexicon*, s.v. "ἄμπελος."

11 David F. Wells, *No Place for Truth* (Grand Rapids: Eerdmans, 1993), 106.

12 T. Hoekstra, *Homiletika*, 172, quoted in **Sidney Greidanus,** *Preaching Christ from the Old Testament* (Grand Rapids: Eerdmans, 1999), 2.

13 Robert G. Rayburn, quoted in **Bryan Chapell,** *Christ-Centered Preaching* (Grand Rapids: Baker, 1994), 17.

14 Graeme Goldsworthy, *Preaching the Whole Bible as Christian Scripture: The Application of Biblical Theology to Expository Preaching* (Grand Rapids: Eerdmans, 2000), 115.

15 D. Martyn Lloyd-Jones, *The Cross: God's Way of Salvation* (Wheaton: Crossway, 1986), viii.

16 Wayne McDill, *The 12 Essential Skills for Great Preaching* (Nashville: Broadman & Holman, 1994), 13.

17 Walter Liefeld, *New Testament Exposition* (Grand Rapids: Zondervan, 1984), 9.

18 Michael Fabarez, *Preaching That Changes Lives* (Nashville: Thomas Nelson, 2002), 112.

19 Donald Grey Barnhouse, quoted in **Michael Horton,** "When the Salt Loses its Savor," accessed August 2007 from www.twoagespilgrims.com/files/show_article.php?id=120HJ.

20 Michael Horton, "Preaching Christ Alone," accessed August 2007 from www.monergism.com/thethreshold/articles/onsite/preachChristalone.html.

21 "To preach the Bible as 'the handbook for life,' or as the answer to every question, rather than as the revelation of Christ, is to turn the Bible into an entirely different book. This is how the Pharisees approached Scripture, however, as we can see clearly from the questions they asked Jesus, all of them amounting to something akin to Trivial Pursuits: 'What happens if a person divorces and remarries?' 'Why do your disciples pick grain on the Sabbath?' 'Who sinned—this man or his parents—that he was born blind?' For the Pharisees, the Scriptures were a source of trivia for life's dilemmas" (**Michael Horton,** "What Are We Looking For in the Bible?" accessed August 2007 from www.modernreformation.org/default.php?page=articledisplay&var1=ArtRead&var2=64&var3=main.

22 Sidney Greidanus, *The Modern Preacher and the Ancient Text: Interpreting and Preaching Biblical Literature* (Grand Rapids: Eerdmans, 1988), 227.

23 Turning descriptive narratives into prescriptions for the church is always a hermeneutical quagmire and should be avoided.

24 Daniel Block, *Judges & Ruth*, New American Commentary (Nashville: Broadman & Holman, 1998), 595.

25 Greidanus, *The Modern Preacher and the Ancient Text*, 220.

26 Bond, *The Master Preacher*, 121.

27 Sinclair B. Ferguson, *Preaching Christ From the Old Testament* (London: The Proclamation Trust, 2002), 3.

28 Chapell, *Christ-Centered Preaching*, 42.

29 Wells, *God in the Wasteland*, 68.

Jesus preached doctrine

The dreaded "d" word is practically a curse or a form of swearing in our postmodern culture. These days, doctrine is derided as vehemently as alcohol was during the days of the temperance movement. Pastors' conventions rarely focus on preaching, let alone doctrinal preaching. Instead, sessions entitled "Encountering God in Solitude and Silence," "How to Read the Culture," and "Designing Emerging Worship Gatherings (That Go Beyond Only Preaching and Singing)"[1] are gobbled up like Thanksgiving dinner. In general, preaching is not embraced, and when firm doctrinal convictions are attached to preaching, the cultural backlash is swift and thorough. Many leaders today treat doctrinal preaching as leprous, giving shouts of "unclean, unclean!" Pastors who are brave enough to teach doctrine are tempted to doctor it up with spoonfuls of sugar to help the big theological words slide down. Doctrinal preaching is not merely frowned upon, it is attacked with aggression. People shudder against and recoil from this incessant pest named "doctrinal preaching."

To further complicate the problem in evangelicalism, many pastors pay lip service to doctrine (they say they believe in it), yet they minimize it from the pulpit, thus denying their actual beliefs. Their methodology betrays their so-called belief in doctrine, as they purposely and systematically jettison deep, meaningful words describing God and His amazing dealings with people. "Simple," "monosyllabic," and "relevance" push thought-provoking concepts such as of the triune and transcendent God out the window. To many, the motto "shallow sells" has pragmatic value, so their pulpits harmoniously chant the well-received refrain, "down with doctrine." Tragically, the congregation adds its antiphonal refrain with glee. Popular preachers buttress their belief in curtailing doctrine with statements such as:

Jesus used simple language. He didn't use technical or theological jargon. He spoke in simple terms that normal people could understand. We need to remember that Jesus did not use the classical Greek language of the scholar ... He used the street language of that day and talked of birds, flowers, lost coins, and other everyday objects that anyone could relate to.[2]

The implication is straightforward: "Pastors, if you want to preach like Jesus, keep it simple, concise, easy, and non-theological. Doctrine is for Bible school, Wednesday night studies, or personal study." Yet, while Jesus was a Man who often spoke simply, hardly anyone, friend or foe, could actually listen to Jesus speak and summarize His preaching as "a-doctrinal."

Doctrine is attacked in other insidious ways. Bishop Gore attempts to neuter Christ's message, saying, "He shrank from making dogmatic statements. Plainly He preferred to stimulate the minds of His disciples to discover the truth (e.g., the truth about Himself) for themselves."[3] My response to "Bishop" Gore would be "rank heresy," "poor anthropology," and that he has a liberal agenda. Gore manifests the recurrent problem of making Jesus into one's own image.

John MacArthur, with his usual precision, identifies the problem and then gives the solution:

But the belief that Christ is against doctrine is a notion I seem to be encountering with increasing frequency. No idea could be much further from the truth. The word doctrine simply means "teaching." And it's ludicrous to say that Christ is anti-teaching. The central imperative of His Great Commission is the command to teach (Matthew 28:18–20). Yet there's no shortage of church-growth experts, professional pollsters, and even seminary professors nowadays who are cautioning young pastors that doctrine is too divisive, too threatening, too heady and theoretical—and therefore simply impractical.[4]

This chapter's purpose is to explore Jesus' doctrinal teaching. You will see that Jesus' teaching was dominated by doctrine. The modern pastor should be settled in his conviction that doctrinal preaching is essential, practical, and relevant. Additionally, congregations must love preaching, especially doctrinal preaching.

Ernest Reisinger's must-read article "The Priority of Doctrinal Preaching" pungently stated, "Jesus was a doctrinal preacher."[5] That sentence shocked me when I first read it. I had to re-read it. The impact of that pithy, five-word sentence came to me with a force similar to that experienced when jumping into the icy ocean without first being allowed to dip your toes or feet in to "measure the water's temperature." Reisinger's title was provocative, but was it true? If it was true—and I believe it was—every pastor should be resolute and determined to emulate the most marvelous Preacher ever! Mark's Gospel furnishes his readers with a picture of that ultimate Preacher. Scripture validates Reisinger's thesis: Jesus broadcasted doctrine.[6] Mark writes,

They went into Capernaum; and immediately on the Sabbath He entered the synagogue and began to teach. They were amazed at His teaching; for He was teaching them as one having authority, and not as the scribes. Just then there was a man in their synagogue with an unclean spirit; and he cried out, saying, "What business do we have with each other, Jesus of Nazareth? Have You come to destroy us? I know who You are—the Holy One of God!" And Jesus rebuked him, saying, "Be quiet, and come out of him!"

Throwing him into convulsions, the unclean spirit cried out with a loud voice and came out of him. They were all amazed, so that they debated among themselves, saying, "What is this? A new teaching with authority! He commands even the unclean spirits, and they obey Him" (Mark 1:21–27).

These listeners in Mark 1:22 were amazed and overwhelmed with Jesus' "teaching" (διδαχῇ). Teaching like this floored the Capernaumites. The King James Version translates "teaching," both in Mark 1:22 and 27, as "doctrine."[7] People were amazed at the doctrine proceeding from Christ. One lexicon lists Mark 1:27 as a description of the doctrinal content of Christ's message, that is to say, Jesus preached substance that contained doctrine.[8] Simply stated, Christ's teaching was doctrinal in nature and in substance. Jesus preached doctrine, and, in the case of Mark 1, it came across as something new that shook the listeners with the resonance of authority.

The Greek word translated "teaching" or "doctrine" can mean more than the basic content of what was taught: it can additionally signify the activity of teaching itself. For example, we read, "And He was teaching them many things in parables, and was saying to them in His teaching ..." (Mark 4:2). The focus here by Mark is not on the content of Jesus' message, but rather on His actual teaching style. Not only did Jesus preach doctrine, but He taught in a doctrinal fashion. Jesus' method of teaching included an intentional aim to teach truths about God and man.

If an outsider were to ask for one descriptive term summarizing the preaching style of Jesus, it would have been "doctrinal." Jesus taught doctrine doctrinally, that is, both the substance and style of His preaching were doctrinal. Jesus preached regularly on topics that would be found in systematic theology books today. He spoke about God the Father (Theology proper), Himself as the Son of God (Christology), the One who would come as Comforter (Pneumatology), the plight of fallen man (Anthropology), God's gracious redemption through ransom (Soteriology), angels, Satan, and demons (Angelology), the end times (Eschatology), and the nature of Holy Scriptures (Bibliology). Each topic is intensely doctrinal and is far from the superficial, watered-down soup that some churches are forced to sup.

Even a cursory survey of the Gospel of Matthew reveals a book stuffed with doctrine:

- Evangelism—Matthew 5:13–16; 10:5–23; 28:18–20
- Bibliology—5:17–20
- Sanctification—5:21–48
- Prayer—6:5–15; 7:7–11
- Pneumatology—12:30–31
- Kingdom of Heaven—13
- Anthropology—15:1–20
- Christology—16:13–20
- Church discipline—18:15–20
- Forgiveness—18:23–35
- Marriage and divorce—19:4–12
- Soteriology (rich young ruler)—19:16–26
- Rewards—19:28–30
- Sovereignty of God—20:1–16
- Sacrificial death of Christ—20:17–19

- Immortality of the soul—22:29–33
- Messiah's lineage—22:41–46
- Exposing false teachers—23
- Eschatology—24–25
- Ecclesiology (in incubator form)—26:26–30; 8:10–12

Are these considered to be doctrines? The answer to that question could be determined by how "doctrine" is defined. Doctrine is anything that explains any truth about God, His universe, or the creatures in said universe. As the King James translators knew, teaching is a perfect synonym for doctrine. Francis Handy understood the grandeur of the Messiah's preaching when he said, "The preaching of Jesus was distinctive for its great themes. It was big preaching, marked by bulk and girth."[9] Paraphrased, Jesus preached big doctrines, and so must you! To say with Raymond Bailey, "Jesus focused on people rather than context. He preached to human needs. Knowledge was a tool to liberate people from destructive ignorance,"[10] is to minimize the truth and to deny the priority of doctrine from Jesus Christ Himself.

Application for preachers, elders, leaders, and Bible teachers

1. PREACH DOCTRINALLY, WITHOUT EXCUSE

Preachers are stewards of God (1 Corinthians 4:1) and must be found trustworthy. All New Testament leaders must answer to the God who has instructed them to teach doctrine. Paul held nothing back when he addressed Titus: "… holding fast the faithful word which is in accordance with the teaching, so that he will be able both to exhort in sound doctrine and to refute those who contradict" (Titus 1:9); "But as for you, speak the things which are fitting for sound doctrine" (Titus 2:1).

If people do not like doctrine, the pastor should not be the influenced but the influencer. The pastor is the leader, and he must lead by teaching truth, which, by definition, divides truth from error. Yes, doctrine does divide—thankfully! Jesus intentionally divided truth and error when He preached. The Pharisees, scribes, and Sadducees all denied that He was the Christ, Israel's Messiah. They did not theologically embrace the doctrines of Jesus' eternal nature, virgin conception, perfect life, substitutionary atonement, or His future resurrection. Jesus assured them of their demise for denying these doctrines.

The controversy surrounding Jesus and His doctrinal preaching should embolden every pastor and leader to obey God and give people sound doctrine, leaving any possibility of hullabaloo to God's providential workings. Leaders, listen to these men who faithfully fought the good fight:

Men tell us that our preaching should be positive and not negative, that we can preach the truth without attacking error. But if we follow that advice we shall have to close our Bible and desert its teachings. The New Testament is a polemic book almost from beginning to end.[11]

Many a preacher has been warned about preaching over the people's heads. I ask, "What are people's heads for? God Almighty gave them those heads and I think they ought to use them!" As a preacher, I deny that any of the truths of God are over the heads of the people. I deny it![12]

There is a familiar story, likely fictional, of a native American Indian who went to church. The sermon he heard was void of spiritual meat and doctrine, but that did not stop the pastor from being loud and boisterous (when preachers know their point is weak, they often raise their voices). The Indian was not moved by the message at all and said of the sermon, "High wind; big thunder; no rain!" Translation: There was nothing substantial or doctrinal contained in the message. Faithful New Testament heralds have no choice but to follow the Lord and His commands in Scripture. Do you preach doctrine?

2. PAY ATTENTION TO YOUR TEACHING

Paul instructed Timothy to give attention to doctrine in 1 Timothy 4:13; then, three verses later (1 Timothy 4:16), he told his son in the faith to pay close attention to doctrine:

Until I come, give attention to the public reading of Scripture, to exhortation and teaching ... Pay close attention to yourself and to your teaching; persevere in these things, for as you do this you will ensure salvation both for yourself and for those who hear you.

What is Paul trying to communicate? All preachers are under the same two present imperatives that bind Timothy. As long as you minister God's Word to God's sheep, you are to pay attention to your teaching. The King James Version translates the word "teaching" in both verses 13 and 16 as "doctrine." This would imply that Paul wants Timothy to have sound doctrine and watch over what is taught. Instead, the lexicons consistently and unanimously articulate the meaning of "teaching" as "the act of teaching or instruction." What does it mean to watch your "act of teaching"? Timothy needed the charge from Paul to be careful with the entire process of preaching, from start to finish. Preparation, prayer, study, resolve, and delivery are all-important and need to be carried out with excellence and under the watchful eye of the Lord. Important as homiletics is to the preacher, he must be concerned with the entire process of teaching.

In verses 13 and 16, two different Greek words are translated "give attention" and "pay close attention." Because the New American Standard Bible translation uses the same word, "attention," for these two different Greek words, the reader might think it is a simple reiteration. Yet Paul purposely uses two different words for more than emphasis. In verse 13, Paul tells Timothy to πρόσεχε ("give heed to," "follow," or "devote oneself to"[13]) his teaching, and in verse 16, he commands him to ἔπεχε ("to take pains," "to give attention to," or "to be mindful of, observant of"[14]) his life and his teaching. Timothy is to be devoted to the teaching of God's Word, and he is also to give solemn attention to his own life. Timothy is under God's mandate to persevere in a holy adherence to God's revealed truth. Obedience in this area affects both Timothy and the congregation entrusted to his care. The stakes for Timothy and the modern pastor could not be higher.

3. REGULARLY TEACH YOUR PEOPLE ABOUT THE IMPORTANCE OF DOCTRINE

Instruct your flock that all of God's Word is "profitable for teaching" (2 Timothy 3:16). In this verse, the word "teaching" is translated "doctrine" in the King James Version. Scripture equips the saints by blending doctrine and duty together. Reisinger held, "Doctrine is to Christian experience what bones are to the body. A body without bones would be an utterly useless lump of 'glob.' Likewise, bones without flesh are but a dead skeleton."[15]

Habitually tell your congregation that doctrine is important. Teach them that it is not abstract, ethereal, boring, or out of date. Educate them about the false bifurcation between "head" and "heart" knowledge for the Bible reader. New Testament readers would consider the heart as a "mission control center" containing much more than an emotional component. Members of the congregation need to understand this biblical concept of the "heart" so that they will understand their need for intellectual doctrine. Affirm publicly the sentiments of Grudem: "Nowhere in Scripture do we find doctrine studied for its own sake or in isolation from life. The biblical writers consistently apply their teaching to life."[16]

4. PURCHASE THE BOOK *THEOLOGICAL "ISM"S*[17] FOR YOUR CHURCH'S BOOK TABLE[18]

A pastor once told the true story of a man who listened to sermons intently. If a word was ever used in the pulpit that was unknown to the man, he would scribble the word down on paper, go home, study the word, and then write a summary paragraph of the doctrinal word. He compiled all the definitions into this marvelous little book, *Theological "ism"s*. I recommend teaching this strategy to your people and/or getting this inexpensive, layman's primer on theology. Soon, your people will not be afraid of big words from the pulpit or Scripture.[19] They are more accustomed to polysyllabic words than you might think. Both hobbies and secular employment come with specialized words that must be memorized and understood.

5. PLACE A "THEOLOGICAL WORD OF THE WEEK" SECTION IN THE SUNDAY BULLETIN

This is a good supplement to solid doctrinal preaching. Get your people comfortable with words that summarize complex scriptural truths. Place one word in your bulletin every week and you will notice people talking about that doctrinal truth.

6. START A BIBLE INSTITUTE AT YOUR CHURCH

College-level classes on the Bible provide your sheep with a great avenue to dig deeper and learn the great truths in the Word. It does not take a lot of work to redo an old seminary syllabus and teach your people hermeneutics, church history, or a theology class. Keep the classes to a six- or seven-week length. You can access an example of a church-based Bible institute on www.bbcchurch.org.

7. PREACH DOCTRINE DIRECTLY TO YOUR PEOPLE

Vague, nebulous preaching is not admirable. The way to the emotions is through the mind. Despite cultural taboos, preach using the second person imperative, "you." "We" preaching is the bane of modern preaching, commonly called "sharing." Initially, your congregation, due to the current evangelical culture, their former pastor's style, or preaching on the radio, may form a perception that you are arrogant, above them, and egotistical. But study Isaiah, Jeremiah, John the Baptist, Jesus, or any apostle, and you will see "you" preaching. George Whitefield was known to preach doctrine so directly that he would often say, "I have come to speak to you about your souls." Obviously, the preacher is not above the congregation, yet he has a message from the King, and he proclaims it for the King in His name. The Scripture passage should be screaming "you" all week to the pastor as he studies, but on Sunday in the pulpit, the preacher, speaking for Another, must say "you" and be as direct as possible.

8. READ WILLIAM PERKINS' *THE ART OF PROPHESYING [PREACHING]*,[20] SPECIFICALLY THE CHAPTER ENTITLED "HOW TO USE AND APPLY DOCTRINE"

This ancient gem is like a Zip drive file in a computer. It is jam-packed with trans-chronological advice from a Puritan preacher who influenced thousands of Puritan preachers.

9. ADORN THE DOCTRINE OF GOD

Paul tells Titus to teach bondslaves to "adorn the doctrine of God our

Savior in every respect" (Titus 2:10). This is also excellent advice for the preacher of doctrine. As you "adorn" the truth of God, the congregation will observe your slow but steady transformation. Your people will not only rejoice in your Christlikeness, they will also emulate your behavior.

10. LET DOCTRINE FLOW NATURALLY OUT OF SEQUENTIAL EXPOSITION

James S. Stewart said, "I think probably the best doctrinal sermons are those which arise in an expository fashion out of the text itself."[21] Scurrying around pell-mell is no way to figure out the next appropriate doctrine to preach. Verse-by-verse teaching will allow the Spirit of God to bring in the next doctrine. Great preachers, such as Martyn Lloyd-Jones and John MacArthur, have no difficulty introducing doctrines on a weekly basis. Why? The Holy Spirit does it for preachers through sequential exposition.

11. REMIND YOUR PEOPLE THAT DOCTRINE IS PRACTICAL

Many congregations hanker for step-by-step, cookbook formulas to "get them by" another week. Gently and regularly instruct your congregation in the importance of soteriology and their position "in Christ." Urge them to affirm the great confession, a miniature statement of faith that reads like a hymn:

By common confession, great is the mystery of godliness:
He who was revealed in the flesh,
Was vindicated in the Spirit,
Seen by angels,
Proclaimed among the nations,
Believed on in the world,
Taken up in glory (1 Timothy 3:16).

The words translated "common confession" are actually from one Greek word, *homologoumenos*. This is an adverb meaning "by consent of all" or "without controversy."[22] Your flock needs to be reminded of the primacy of soteriology before practical living, because practical application flows from their position in Christ.

When doctrine is taught as practical, it will be seen as a benefit and received warmly. The Heidelberg Catechism demonstrated the practical nature of doctrine, with the authors placing at the end of every doctrinal section the question "How does this comfort you?" On your dying day, you will rely strictly on truths about the Godhead for your hope. John DeBrine once shared with me the story of his heart attack. He said, "When I was lying on the ground during my heart attack, I was not singing, 'Shine, Jesus, shine.' I was saying to myself, 'My hope is built on nothing less than Jesus' blood and righteousness.'"[23] Strong doctrinal foundations undergird the Christian in the most extreme trials. The great Scottish preacher John Knox, on his deathbed and unable to speak, responded to a servant's question with nonverbal doctrine. The attendant asked Knox to raise his hand as a sign that the gospel Knox preached his whole life was currently comforting him, so close to glory. Knox lifted his hand three times to signify emphatic agreement. Machen, on his deathbed, sent a telegram to his colleague John Murray that read, "I'm so thankful for the active obedience of Christ. No hope without it." Doctrine—no hope without it.

Conversely, coach your flock to see that weak doctrines get pulverized by the weight of powerful temptations. Sin and temptation must be refuted by truths of God that are anchored in the Scriptures, especially the doctrine of the person and nature of God. Understanding the unchanging, eternal, powerful, kind, and holy God will help your congregation see everything in its proper perspective. When trials are at their most severe, only solid, well-founded doctrines support the weary Christian. Doctrine serves as the scaffolding for weary saints in trouble. When strong temptations attack the Christian, he or she must have a foundation of strong, well-founded truths about God in order to resist the flesh.

12. PROTECT YOUR FLOCK BY TEACHING DOCTRINE

Train your people to grasp the consequences of believing wrong doctrine. Paul knew that Timothy needed to grasp the ramifications of following men who abandon the ship of sound doctrine:

But the Spirit explicitly says that in later times some will fall away from the faith, paying attention to deceitful spirits and doctrines of demons, by means of the hypocrisy of liars seared in their own conscience as with a branding iron, men who forbid marriage and advocate abstaining from foods which God has created to be gratefully shared in by those who believe and know the truth. For everything created by God is good, and nothing is to be rejected if it is received with gratitude (1 Timothy 4:1–4).

John MacArthur portrays this scene, saying, "In other words, lying, hypocrisy, a dulled conscience, and false religious practices all have root in wrong doctrine."[24] False doctrine is more easily seen against the backdrop of healthy, hygienic doctrine.

Application for laypeople and congregations

1. PICK ONE "OLOGY" EVERY YEAR AND STUDY IT THOROUGHLY

Chose a biblical subject that interests you and dive into learning it. If you need a starting place, *soteriology*, the doctrine of salvation, would be a good place to begin. Next year, move on to the next "ology," and in ten years you will be well on your way to a thorough examination of biblical doctrine and the Scriptures that support it. If you are web-savvy, www.monergism.com is a full-service theological website that is evangelical and conservative in nature. Another option is to buy "systematic theology" books. These "systematize" the entire Bible, from Genesis to Revelation, addressing particular topics. They present what the entire Bible teaches about a doctrine. Get recommendations from your church leaders.

2. BUDGET SOME MONEY FOR A THEOLOGICAL LIBRARY THAT WILL LAST A LIFETIME

Ask your pastor for his "top ten" books to start your resource library. Think of it as a theological investment for your family. Watch out for best-selling Christian books in your local bookstore because most Christian bookstores have little or no theological discernment. You cannot always judge a Christian book by its cover! Stick with reputable authors and publishers.

3. BE COGNIZANT OF WHAT COMES OUT OF THE PULPIT

Be aware of what comes out of the pulpit and what does not. A sure sign that doctrine is on the way out at your church is when other substances fill the gap left by its absence. When biblical doctrine goes out, something must replace it because nothing is done in a vacuum. Especially watch out for psychology replacing God-centered doctrine. John MacArthur warns of the danger of replacing doctrine with psychology, saying, "But if there is a deficiency in preaching today, it is that there's too much relational, pseudo-psychological, and thinly life-related content, and not enough emphasis on sound doctrine."[25] Be alert to other current fads intruding on the pulpit, such as the latest business techniques emanating from trendy leadership gurus. Be Bereans and examine everything according to the Scriptures.

4. REJOICE IN KNOWING THAT DOCTRINE DIVIDES

Be glad about this! Jesus purposely used doctrine to divide truth from error and righteousness from unrighteousness. Jesus preached doctrine to the self-righteous Pharisees so they could understand their spiritual depravity and the proper doctrine of the Messiah. If there must be a controversy, let Bible preaching start and finish it.

5. STRIVE FOR HUMILITY AS YOUR DOCTRINE INCREASES AND IS REFINED

Remember that doctrine is as essential to the Christian as a skeleton is to a human body, but continue to "flesh out" your doctrine as you prayerfully incorporate into your life what you have learned (doctrine should lead to duty; creed should find its goal in conduct). Two scholars give good warnings to proud theologians or congregational members:

In the study of all other sciences man places himself *above* the object of his investigation and *actively* elicits from it his knowledge by whatever method may seem most appropriate, but in theology he does not stand above but rather *under* the object of his knowledge (Louis Berkhof).[26]

Self-righteousness can feed upon doctrines, as well as upon works; and a man may have the heart of a Pharisee, while his head is stored with orthodox notions of the unworthiness of the creature and the riches of free grace (John Newton).[27]

Notes

1 I must refrain from digressing to discuss the modern trend of Roman Catholic mysticism that

is rampant in evangelical circles and how it assaults the sufficiency of Scripture and, eventually, the proclamation of the Word.

2 **Rick Warren,** "A Primer on Preaching Like Jesus, Part One," accessed June 2007 from www.cbn.com/spirituallife/churchandministry/warren_preach_like_jesusa.aspx.

3 **Bishop Gore,** in **Donald Baillie,** *God Was In Christ: An Essay on Incarnation and Atonement* (New York: Charles Scribner's Sons, 1948), 101–102.

4 **John MacArthur,** "Doctrine is Practical," accessed July 2007 from phillipjohnson.blogspot.com/2005/12/another-guest-post-from-my-favorite.html.

5 **Ernest Reisinger,** "The Priority of Doctrinal Preaching," accessed June 2007 from www.founders.org/FJ23/article2.html.

6 Too often, pastors relegate Mark's Gospel as the "Action Gospel" and skip over the importance of Jesus' preaching in this Synoptic.

7 The full verses in the KJV read: "And they were astonished at his doctrine: for he taught them as one that had authority, and not as the scribes" (Mark 1:22); "And they were all amazed, insomuch that they questioned among themselves, saying, What thing is this? what new doctrine is this? for with authority commandeth he even the unclean spirits, and they do obey him" (Mark 1:27).

8 *BDAG*, s.v. "διδαχῇ." This lexicon says this work contains both the "activity of teaching" and "the content of teaching."

9 **Francis J. Handy,** *Jesus the Preacher* (New York: Abingdon-Cokesbury Press, 1946), 118.

10 **Raymond Bailey,** *Jesus the Preacher* (Nashville: Broadman Press, 1990), 45.

11 **J. Gresham Machen,** lecture delivered in London on June 17, 1932, accessed August 2007 from jmm.aaa.net.au/articles/15133.htm.

12 Attributed to **Benjamin Breckenridge Warfield,** accessed August 2007 from biblicalchristian.wordpress.com.

13 **F. Wilbur Gingrich,** *Shorter Lexicon of the Greek New Testament*, 2nd ed., ed. **F. Wilbur Gingrich** and **Frederick William Danker** (Chicago: The University of Chicago Press, 1965) in *Bible Works* [CD-ROM] (Norfolk: BibleWorks LLC, 1992–2003), s.v. "προσέχω."

14 *BDAG*, s.v. "ἐπέχω."

15 **Reisinger,** "The Priority of Doctrinal Preaching."

16 **Wayne Grudem,** *Systematic Theology* (Grand Rapids: Zondervan, 1994), 23.

17 **Randy Smith,** *Theological "ism"s: A Layman's Reference Guide to Selected Theological Terms* (Southlake, TX: Countryside Institute for Biblical Studies, 1999).

18 If you do not have a book table of some sort, you should! It is imperative that you have a variety of books for sale at the church. Make sure you pick the authors, titles, and subjects

until you have discipled someone to attend to the ministry. I recommend that you have no profit margin as a church, counting the maturation of your saints as profit instead.

19 Every job in the world employs words that are large, acronyms that are complex, or jargon. Your people will quickly enjoy learning.

20 William Perkins, *The Art of Prophesying* (Carlisle, PA: Banner of Truth, 1996).

21 James S. Stewart, "Expository Preaching: Preaching from Doctrine" (lecture delivered at Union Theological Seminary, Richmond, VA., August 1955).

22 *Thayer's Lexicon*, s.v. "ὁμολογουμένως."

23 Personal conversation in West Boylston, MA, 1997.

24 MacArthur, "Doctrine Is Practical."

25 Ibid.

26 Louis Berkhof, *Systematic Theology* (Grand Rapids: Eerdmans, 1996), 34.

27 John Newton, "A Guide to Godly Disputation." Accessed from www.thirdmill.org/files/english/practical_theology/18074%7E7_12_02_9-33-28_AM%7EPT.Newton.godly.disputation.pdf [page 3].

Jesus preached as a herald

"**D**o not preach to me" is the motto of today's culture. Today's society, which disdains the idea of preaching, has had many negative influences. You can hear the world shouting with emphasis, "Who are *you* to tell *me* what to do?" Modern definitions of preaching betray the negative views held about it: that preaching contains some kind of moralizing message that intrudes into someone's personal and private life. An online dictionary gives one definition of preaching as "somebody giving advice on morals: somebody who gives advice on morality or behavior in an irritatingly tedious or overbearing way."[1] Consequently, preaching in general is going the way of the horse and cart, with "participatory learning" or "nonlinear learning" becoming the preferred form of communication. Many congregations want multiple voices heard, complete with time for questions, comments, and exploration, as a replacement to what they see as one preacher's voice dominating "the conversation" with a monolithic monopoly.

The best illustration I know of people's rejection for valiant, strong preaching comes from a Bible conference in India at which I spoke. Another speaker, through a live video link, was John MacArthur, and he was actually preaching from the United States. John, with his typical boldness and clarity, was proclaiming to the conference attendees the narrowness of the gospel, its parameters, and its exclusivity. As he spoke, his image was projected onto a large screen on the stage. I was seated in the front row, not by choice but because of cultural norms, and, out of the corner of my eye, I spied a man staggering, wobbling up to the front platform area. My first thought was to get up and assist the man. Suddenly, the man climbed up, and with epileptic-like strokes, slammed the projector screen with John's image on it down to the ground. For a moment, I thought the man was physically ill. That idea quickly receded as I watched the next few moments of slow-motion, freeze-frame drama. The man began to forcefully stomp his feet on the video screen, the screen that, to him, represented John MacArthur and his message from the Bible. Of course, John could not see this. The camera was in front of the man (I told John the story later). In surreal fashion, John's voice just kept bellowing out over the sound system despite the angry man's incessant stomping. John's image was no longer seen, but his voice was not so easily muted. Quickly, the local Indian elders "escorted" the man away (interestingly, the man had earlier been selling Benny Hinn books in the parking lot—without authorization!). This scene has been engraved in my mind as a picture of fallen man's response to the herald's proclamation of the Word of God.

Many ministers today have compromised their God-given responsibility to be heralds because of the pressure they are experiencing. Dogmatic "thus says the LORD" proclamations have been replaced with "sharing times," replete with subtle nuances that would soothe any fidgety kindergarten student anticipating "snack time." Pastors are judged by congregants on perceived warmth, kind delivery, and the fact that they do not "preach down to the people." In earlier eras, preachers were rated by doctrinal fidelity, biblical precision, and passion for a transcendent view of God's greatness. Today, people judge their pastors on niceness, kindness, and perceived warmth of personality.

Catching the spirit of the age is not admirable, nor does it resemble the ministry of Jesus Christ. This chapter intends to bolster the confidence of expositors by observing the heralding ministry of the Lord. I believe a cursory glance at the *modus operandi* of Jesus will cause the compromising pastor to quickly jettison any dialogical format that he currently employs. People may have a derogatory perception of second person imperative preaching ("you," not "we"), but Jesus Christ, as God's Son and messenger, trumpeted the gospel of His Father's kingdom without shame. He did so as a herald of the King. This chapter will also encourage the pastor who is currently forth-telling God's gospel of grace to continue to herald the Word in the manner of His Master Jesus Christ.

Robert H. Mounce, in his excellent book *The Essential Nature of New Testament Preaching*, asserts, "The portrayal of Jesus in the Synoptic Gospels is supremely that of one who came 'heralding the kingdom of God.' This characteristic phase of Jesus' ministry is represented by the verb *kerussein* more than twenty times."[2] Jesus was God's herald. He proclaimed the gospel with boldness. The context of Matthew 4 sees Jesus beginning His ministry. Matthew says:

Now when Jesus heard that John had been taken into custody, He withdrew into Galilee; and leaving Nazareth, He came and settled in Capernaum, which is by the sea, in the region of Zebulun and Naphtali. This was to fulfill what was spoken through Isaiah the prophet:

"The land of Zebulun and the land of Naphtali,
By the way of the sea, beyond the Jordan, Galilee of the Gentiles—
The people who were sitting in darkness saw a great Light,
And those who were sitting in the land and shadow of death,
Upon them a Light dawned."

From that time Jesus began to preach and say, "Repent, for the kingdom of heaven is at hand" (Matthew 4:12–17).

From that time Jesus began His preaching ministry (Matthew 4:17), and He never stopped it. "Began" signifies the start of an ongoing process. Preaching defined the Savior's mission, from the inauguration of His public ministry to His death on a cross. Heralding so epitomized the Messiah's role that scholar Mounce said, "It [proclamation] serves as a résumé of His ministry."[3] Jesus' public ministry could be summed up in one word: heralding. Technically, the infinitive "to preach" in Matthew 4:17 is in the Greek a present active (κηρύσσειν), indicating continuation and the durative nature of the announcement. The lexicons are uniform in their description of this word. BDAG depicts "preach" as "to make an official announcement, announce, make known and, secondly, to make public declarations, proclaim aloud."[4] Another lexicon says this verb is "most often in reference to God's saving action."[5] Jesus, with "hear ye, hear ye" force, preaches to people, even at people. Jesus is vested with God the Father's full authority, and He summons the people with the King's message.

Jesus initiates His lifelong mission of spreading the story of repentance and the kingdom of heaven. God's Son, as official herald, widely disseminates His Father's decree. Whereas John the Baptist had limited scope with his message of repentance (people came to him where he was), Jesus expands the extent of the good news into new areas and to many other people. Matthew goes on to say more of this expansive heralding:

Jesus was going throughout all Galilee, teaching in their synagogues and proclaiming the gospel of the kingdom, and healing every kind of disease and every kind of sickness among the people (Matthew 4:23).

The Greek language of Matthew 4:23 demonstrates an ongoing proclamation[6] and gives the readers a summary of the pre-Calvary life of Christ. Far beyond Capernaum, Jesus invaded the nooks and crannies of Israel with the gospel of God. John the Baptist's ministry was typified by proclaiming repentance to a small geographic area; Jesus proclaimed repentance (negative side of the message) and the gospel of the kingdom (positive side) throughout all of northern Israel. His announcement was simple: "There is good news from the King, for the King Himself declares it."

Notice that Matthew did not say Jesus "shared" or "dialogued" or that He engaged in any kind of "group think" abounding with moral platitudes. Why? Because the role of the herald forbids it! The herald represents another, someone else who has a higher authority. The Greek noun form of "heralding" is *keryx,* and it lends insight about Jesus' role as herald, expanding our conception of what Jesus did. A herald was "a messenger vested with ... authority, who conveyed the official messages of kings, magistrates, princes, military commanders, or who gave a public summons or demand, and performed various other duties."[7] Heralds give out information in a one-directional approach.

I did not excel at trumpet practice in middle school, but I did very quickly understand that the trumpet mouthpiece was meant to have air blown into it. Inhalation would produce no sound at all, at least, not a musical sound (it also filled your mouth full of old saliva left in the trumpet—yuck). Similar to a trumpet player, the herald sounds forth a public summons that beckons people to listen and obey. Heralds "exhale" God's demands and they trumpet forth the Lord's Word. Jesus, as herald, called for His audience to listen and obey God's Word. He told His listeners His Father's will with public announcements. As God the Father's incarnate ambassador, Jesus proclaimed the will of God in perfect obedience to the Father. To speak anything more, or less, would be disobedient to the role of proclaimer of the King.

Jesus, and all heralds who would follow Him, needed to speak with authority. Tracing the background of the meaning of the word "herald" yields insight to this authority:

In the ancient world a "herald" was the person who by order of a superior made a loud, public announcement. Thus, in public games it was his function to announce the name and country of each competitor, and also the name, country, and father of the victor ... The picture is beautiful. It is not the rebellious city which sends out an ambassador to sue for peace-terms, but the offended King of kings who sends his own herald to proclaim peace through a ransom, and that ransom: the blood of his own dear Son![8]

Everything that the herald did pointed to getting the people's attention and calling for obedience. The herald knew how critical it was for his audience to listen.[9] The call to heed the herald can be seen in several biblical examples:

1. An angel: "And I saw a strong angel proclaiming with a loud voice, 'Who is worthy to open the book and to break its seals?'" (Revelation 5:2).
2. A healed man: "And he went away and began to proclaim in Decapolis what great things Jesus had done for him; and everyone was amazed" (Mark 5:20).
3. Nebuchadnezzar's herald: "Then the herald loudly proclaimed: 'To you the command is given, O peoples, nations and men of every language, that at the moment you hear the sound of the horn, flute, lyre, trigon, psaltery, bagpipe and all kinds of music, you are to fall down and worship the golden image that Nebuchadnezzar the king has set up'" (Daniel 3:4–5).
4. God instructing Jonah to herald: "Arise, go to Nineveh the great city and cry against it, for their wickedness has come up before Me" (Jonah 1:2); "Arise, go to Nineveh the great city and proclaim to it the proclamation which I am going to tell you"[10] (Jonah 3:2).

5. John the Baptist: "He said, 'I am a voice of one crying in the wilderness, "Make straight the way of the LORD," as Isaiah the prophet said'" (John 1:23).

Extensive distribution is the herald's goal. Today's marketing gurus discuss market saturation and penetration with motives that are not always altruistic. Biblical heralds must, with fidelity, give "earnest proclamation of news initiated by God"[11] to as many people as God providentially allows. Heralds put aside their own views and opinions and proclaim God's Word without debate, excuse, or shame to the widest possible audience.

Application for preachers, elders, leaders, and Bible teachers

1. PREACH AS IF YOU ARE SENT BY A MONARCH—
BECAUSE YOU *WERE* SENT BY THE KING OF KINGS

Pastors today must follow Jesus' example as they herald His Word. The words of 2 Timothy 4:2 ("preach the word") make heralding nonnegotiable for all who dare to speak for God. In 2 Timothy 4, Paul is essentially saying to Timothy, "Be like Jesus and proclaim the Word as a herald!"[12] The three words "preach the word" carry the theological, if not the grammatical, stress of 2 Timothy 4. These words are the key to the whole passage. With crisp, military-like orders, Paul commands Timothy to take his commission seriously and to fulfill it by announcing all of the King's message. There has been too much "worldly and empty chatter" (1 Timothy 6:20) in the church, and Timothy is not to contribute to any "so-called knowledge." Neither are you.

2. PREACH IN SUCH A WAY THAT YOU POST NOTICE
ON YOUR CONGREGATION'S MINDS

All Bible preachers act like town criers in medieval England, who

were the chief means of news communication with the people of the town since many people could not read or write. Royal proclamations, local bylaws, market days, adverts, even selling loaves of sugar were all proclaimed by a bellman or crier throughout the centuries ... A little-known fact is that the term "Posting A Notice" actually comes from the act of the Town Crier, who having read his message to the Townspeople, would attach it to the door post of the local Inn or Tavern.[13]

Preaching should be carried out in such a way as to permanently engrave His Word in the minds of a pastor's listeners. Like Timothy, your Superior has authorized your message, and you are to forcefully declare it to others. Let's look at the well-known passage on preaching (2 Timothy 4) through the lens of heralding and see six ways in which you should "preach the word."

How should you herald?

YOU MUST HERALD SOBERLY

Paul starts this chapter with serious, courtroom language. The gravity and soberness of this "you are under oath" language is unparalleled in Scripture outside of Paul's epistles to Timothy.[14] Paul says,

I solemnly charge you in the presence of God and of Christ Jesus, who is to judge the living and the dead, and by His appearing and His kingdom (2 Timothy 4:1).

Paul charges you, through Timothy, with an order from God on high. In God's law court, Paul's responsibility is to earnestly testify for Him. This is so serious it should mark your life indelibly. "Charge"[15] in Greek is defined as follows:

To make a solemn declaration about the truth of something, testify of, bear witness to (orig. under oath) … to exhort with authority in matters of extraordinary importance, freq. w. ref. to higher powers and/or suggestion of peril, solemnly urge, exhort, warn … to state something in such a way that the auditor is to be impressed with its seriousness.[16]

God, the judging God who will judge you, has given you strict orders to preach. Paul, on his "deathbed," is concerned that Timothy preach to others before an audience of the Trinity. Matthew Henry said, "the eye of God and Jesus Christ was upon him."[17] Many admire C.H. Spurgeon, but how many emulate his soberness?

There is not a Sunday night when I do not come on this platform in such a state, both of body and soul, that I pity a dog who has to suffer what I have, under the terror and the weight of the awful responsibility of having to preach to such a crowd as this ... Before I come to address the congregation in this tabernacle, I tremble like an aspen leaf. And often, in coming down to this pulpit, have I felt my knees knock together—not that I am afraid of any one of my hearers, but I am thinking of that account which I must render to God, whether I speak His Word faithfully or not ... My deacons know well enough how, when I first preached in Exeter Hall, there was scarcely ever an occasion in which they left me alone for 10 minutes before the service, but they would find me in a most fearful state of sickness, produced by that tremendous thought of my solemn responsibility.[18]

The King's herald must be sober as he preaches the Word, because God is watching.

YOU MUST HERALD FAITHFULLY

I once heard MacArthur say, "Men, early in your ministry decide this: do you want to be faithful or popular? You can only choose one." If the King has appointed you to herald the Word, then by all means be faithful. Paul told Timothy to preach the Word and "be ready in season and out of season" (2 Timothy 4:2). Are you ready, willing, and able to preach at all times and in all places? The Phillips Bible translates Paul's instructions as "never lose your sense of urgency," but the text points more to a constant duty, like that seen in a soldier who is always on his guard or stays at his post or station. John Calvin agreed, saying, "By these words he recommends not only constancy, but likewise earnestness, so as to overcome all hindrances and difficulties; for, being, by nature, exceedingly effeminate or slothful, we easily yield to the slightest opposition, and sometimes we gladly seek apologies for our slothfulness."[19] All seasons are appropriate for heralding. Pastors have a green light to declare God's counsel on all matters and at all times.

I once met a local pastor and asked him my diagnostic question for pastors: "Which book of the Bible are you currently preaching?" This question zeroes in on whether pastors preach with sequential exposition. His response was shocking: "Sometimes the Lord leads me not to preach in the worship service." I was stupefied. I really cannot remember how I responded. I wanted to say, "I don't know what 'lord' led you not to preach, but his name was not Jesus." Thankfully, this man is no longer a pastor.

YOU MUST HERALD AUTHORITATIVELY

As a pastor, you have the full authority of a herald. You need not pine away for it: you already have it. Your authority is a delegated authority, but it still gives you the right to preach. Paul says that your preaching should contain reproving, rebuking, and exhorting (2 Timothy 4:2). A.W. Tozer said, "We are not diplomats but prophets, and our message is not a compromise but an ultimatum."[20] Tozer's words convey the proper sense of "reprove, rebuke, exhort." Your authority must call people to moments of crisis. You can read music books but they do not command you to perform sonatas. Cookbooks are interesting, but they do not force you to make chocolate chip cookies.

The current fascination of preaching "as one without authority"[21] paints a seemingly nice picture, but not of a New Testament herald. Albert Mohler understands the mandate of preaching and the clout it must carry: "If we have no authoritative message, why preach?"[22]

There are three components to preaching with authority:

1. You have the authority to reprove. Reproof lets the congregation identify what sin is and what it is not. Convincingly you inform the mind and assist the listeners to properly understand what God's Word says about sin. After the congregation is aware of sin, you may take the next step.
2. You have the authority to rebuke. Rebuke attaches ownership to the sin that was just reproved. It convicts the sinner by attaching personal blame. Guilt is affixed to the individual. Reproof says, "This is sin," while rebuke states, "You are the man." The following quotes describe rebuke perfectly:

The honest preacher calls a sin a sin, and a spade a spade, and says to men, "You are ruining yourselves; while you reject Christ you are living on the borders of hell, and ere long you will be lost to all eternity. There shall be no mincing the matter, you must escape from the wrath to come by faith in Jesus, or be driven for ever from God's presence, and from all hope of joy." The preacher must make his sermons cut. He is not to file off the edge of his scythe for fear it should hurt somebody. No, my hearers, we mean to hurt you; our sickle is made on purpose to cut. The gospel is intended to wound the conscience, and to go right through the heart, with the design of separating the soul from sin and self, as the corn is divided from the soil. Our object is to cut the sinner right down, for all the comeliness of the flesh must be slain, all his glory, all his excellence must be withered, and the man must be as one dead ere he can be saved. Ministers who do not aim to cut deep are not worth their salt. God never sent the man who never troubles men's consciences. Such a man may be an ass treading down the corn, but a reaper he certainly is not. We want faithful ministers; pray God to send them. Ask him to give us men who will preach the whole truth, who will not be afraid of certain humbling doctrines, but will bring out, for instance, the doctrine of election, and not be ashamed of it, who will tell men that salvation is of the Lord, and will not go about to please them by letting them have a finger in salvation, as though they were to share in the glory of it. Oh for laborers who can use sharp cutting sickles upon ungodly hearts!" (Spurgeon)[23]

Some preachers remind me of the famous Chinese jugglers ... one of these stood against a wall, and the other threw knives at him. One knife would be driven into the board just above his head, and another close by his ear, while under his armpit and between his fingers quite a number of deadly weapons were bristling. Wonderful art to be able to throw to a hair's breadth and never strike! How many among us have a marvelous skill in missing! "Be not afraid," says the preacher, "I am never personal. I never give home-thrusts." Stand quite still, my friend! Open your arms! Spread your fingers! Your minister has practiced a very long while, and he knows how to avoid troubling you in the least with truth too severely personal. Brethren, cultivate that art if you desire to be damned, and wish your hearers also to be lost; but if you want to be the means of saving both yourselves and them that hear you, cry to your Lord for faithfulness, practicalness, real heart-moving power. Never play at preaching nor beat about the bush; get at it, and always mean business (Spurgeon).[24]

Socrates, I hate you, because every time I meet you, you make me see what I am (Alcibiades).[25]

It is a poor sermon that gives no offense, that neither makes the hearer displeased with himself nor with the preacher (Whitefield).[26]

Preach so that if people don't hate their sin, they will hate you (Luther).[27]

Many a meandering discourse one hears, in which the preacher aims at nothing, and— hits it (Whately).[28]

3. You have the authority to exhort. Exhortation is the urging and begging of sinners to stop their behavior and positively look to the forgiving Lord. While "reprove" and "rebuke" are negative in nature, "exhort" is positive. This manner of exhortation was shown by Paul to the Thessalonians: "Just as you know how we were exhorting and encouraging and imploring each one of you as a father would his own children" (1 Thessalonians 2:11).

YOU MUST HERALD PATIENTLY
Next, Paul tells his protégé to preach with "great patience" (2 Timothy 4:2). Patient preaching remains steady with a forbearing love for God's people. Most often, "patience" is a word that tells of God's forbearance. As God has been patient with you, be longsuffering with His people as you preach to them. If they understood what you preached as fast as you grasped, they would have been the ones in seminary, not you.

Patient preaching waits on the Lord to give the increase, sanctify His people, and produce fruit that human manipulation could never accomplish. The route of high-pressure sales pitches is in direct contradiction to the tenor of Paul's exhortation. God blesses His Word and promises to work through it:

So will My word be which goes forth from My mouth;
It will not return to Me empty,
Without accomplishing what I desire,
And without succeeding in the matter for which I sent it (Isaiah 55:11).

As a preacher, keep serving the meal God has prepared with patience and kindness. Yes, you have already taught your people these same truths, but much of preaching is reminding people of what they already know. The words "remind" and "remember" are so often listed in the epistles that it is frankly frightening to think that we are so forgetful:

REMIND

But I have written very boldly to you on some points, so as to *remind* you again, because of the grace that was given me from God (Romans 15:15).

For this reason I have sent to you Timothy, who is my beloved and faithful child in the Lord, and he will *remind* you of my ways which are in Christ, just as I teach everywhere in every church (1 Corinthians 4:17).

For this reason I *remind* you to kindle afresh the gift of God which is in you through the laying on of my hands (2 Timothy 1:6).

Remind them of these things, and solemnly charge them in the presence of God not to wrangle about words, which is useless and leads to the ruin of the hearers (2 Timothy 2:14).

Remind them to be subject to rulers, to authorities, to be obedient, to be ready for every good deed (Titus 3:1).

Therefore, I will always be ready to *remind* you of these things, even though you already know them, and have been established in the truth which is present with you (2 Peter 1:12).

Now I desire to *remind* you, though you know all things once for all, that the Lord, after saving a people out of the land of Egypt, subsequently destroyed those who did not believe (Jude 5).

REMEMBER

Therefore *remember*, that formerly you, the Gentiles in the flesh, who are called "Uncircumcision" by the so-called "Circumcision," which is performed in the flesh by human hands—*remember* that you were at that time separate from Christ, excluded from the commonwealth of Israel, and strangers to the covenants of promise, having no hope and without God in the world (Ephesians 2:11–12).

Do you not *remember* that while I was still with you, I was telling you these things? (2 Thessalonians 2:5).

Remember Jesus Christ, risen from the dead, descendant of David, according to my gospel (2 Timothy 2:8).

… that you should *remember* the words spoken beforehand by the holy prophets and the commandment of the Lord and Savior spoken by your apostles (2 Peter 3:2).

But you, beloved, ought to *remember* the words that were spoken beforehand by the apostles of our Lord Jesus Christ (Jude 17).

Be patient when it comes to your congregation's spiritual growth. Do not expect to see tangible growth weekly. Just as children grow slowly, so too do spiritual children.

YOU MUST HERALD DOCTRINALLY[29]

In 2 Timothy 4 Paul goes on to say that preaching must be with "instruction." As we have already seen in Chapter 4 ("Jesus preached doctrine"), doctrinal teaching is mandatory. Anyone saying, "I do not believe in doctrine; I believe only in Jesus," misunderstands that doctrine is teaching or instruction about God.

How important was doctrine to the New Testament church? Acts 2:42 says, "They were continually devoting themselves to the apostles' teaching and to fellowship, to the breaking of bread and to prayer." Doctrine is important. Listen to Brooks:

The truth is, no preaching ever had any strong power that was not the preaching of doctrine. The preachers that have moved and held men have always preached doctrine. No exhortation to a good life that does not put behind it some truth as deep as eternity can seize and hold the conscience. Preach doctrine, preach all the doctrine that you know, and learn forever more and more; but preach it always, not that men may believe it, but that they may be saved by believing it.[30]

YOU MUST HERALD COURAGEOUSLY

When you preach God's Word, you will face opposition. People will attack the message first, then you, the messenger. I personally have been called "Stalin," "Hitler," and "The Uni-Bomber" (my favorite). Preachers must "act like men" since they herald in a wicked time, described in 2 Timothy 4:3–4:

For the time will come when they will not endure sound doctrine; but wanting to have their ears tickled, they will accumulate for themselves teachers in accordance to their own desires, and will turn away their ears from the truth and will turn aside to myths.

In every period of history, there are groups refusing to accept sound doctrine. They despise and hate it, echoing Isaiah 30:10 (KJV), "Speak unto us smooth things, prophesy deceits." G. Campbell Morgan corrected a common adage of his day, "The preacher must catch the spirit of the age," saying, "God forgive him if he does. The preacher's business is to correct the spirit of the age." You must preach even when people will not endure or tolerate God's good news. Stand firm when people, with mouths thirsty from the salt of sin, hanker for unhealthy, unspiritual words that tickle instead of convict. Depressingly, there are plenty of false teachers to go around for all. Just as ants are drawn to sugar or as drone bees zoom to the queen, so false teachers are as magnets to the sinful metal of people's hearts. Listen to Calvin's wisdom:

We should note the word "heap" ["accumulate"] by which he means that their madness will be so great that they will not be content with a few impostors but will want a great crowd. As there is always an insatiable desire for vain and harmful things, the world seeks on every side and without limit all the means of its own destruction it can devise and imagine, and the devil always has available as many teachers of this kind as the world requires. There has always been a plenteous harvest of wicked men, as there is today, and Satan has never any lack of helpers or of means for deceiving men.[31]

SUMMARY
As you, by the Spirit's enablement, preach the Word, you will be following both Christ's command and example. It is well worth the trouble.

Application for laypeople and congregations

1. DO NOT EXPECT YOUR PASTOR TO APOLOGIZE FOR BEING A HERALD

The gospel herald should spend his time preaching accurately and boldly. Do not make him waste a moment of time apologizing for his high calling and what it contains.

2. UNDERSTAND THE PLACE OF THE PULPIT IN THE CHURCH

In the old days, preachers would ascend the pulpit and speak to God's people as if God Himself were speaking. Modern buildings where churches gather do not normally allow a high pulpit, but the pulpit can be placed in the center of the church to signify importance, centrality, and focus.

3. UNDERSTAND YOUR PASTOR PRIMARILY AS "THE PREACHER" AND NOT "REVEREND," "PASTOR," OR ANY OTHER NAME FOR CLERGY

In our society, titles and names still convey what a person does. Call your pastor "preacher" and watch him smile.

4. REGULARLY READ THE OLD TESTAMENT PROPHETS AND STUDY THEIR LANGUAGE OF PROCLAMATION

Reading the Bible will reinforce the urgency and intensity found in God's herald.

5. READ *THE FEMINIZATION OF AMERICAN CULTURE* BY ANN DOUGLAS[32]

Ann Douglas does not profess to be an evangelical Christian, but she does understand the effects of feminism on Christianity. This eye-opening book documents how feminism filled the vacuum that non-Calvinistic preaching created.

6. PRAY THAT YOUR PASTOR NEVER GETS CREATIVE IN THE PULPIT

R.L. Dabney said, "The preacher is a herald; his work is heralding the

King's message … Now the herald does not invent his message; he merely transmits and explains it."[33] There is no room for creativity or being novel in either interpretation or application. You want your pastor to continue in the systematic, faithful delivery of the "old, old story."

7. REMEMBER THE DIFFERENCE BETWEEN PREACHING AND TEACHING

There are many technical definitions that delineate the teaching and preaching distinction. The best way to think about them is that teaching imparts information, while preaching imparts information using passionate exhortation with an eye to honoring Jesus Christ with obedience. John Stott describes the difference, saying,

Heralding is not the same as lecturing. A lecture is dispassionate, objective, academic. It is addressed to the mind. It seeks no result but to impart certain information and, perhaps, to provoke the student to further enquiry. But the herald of God comes with an urgent proclamation of peace through the blood of the cross, and with a summons to men to repent, to lay down their arms and humbly to accept the offered pardon.[34]

Notes

1 *Encarta Online English Dictionary*, North American Edition, accessed June 2007 from encarta.msn.com/encnet/features/dictionary/DictionaryResults.aspx?refid=1861737453.

2 **Robert H. Mounce,** *The Essential Nature of New Testament Preaching* (Eugene, OR: Wipf & Stock, 1960), 28.

3 Ibid.

4 *BDAG*, s.v. "κηρύσσω."

5 **F. Wilbur Gingrich,** *Shorter Lexicon of the Greek New Testament*, 2nd ed., ed. **F. Wilbur Gingrich** and **Frederick William Danker** (Chicago: The University of Chicago Press, 1965) in *Bible Works* [CD-ROM] (Norfolk: BibleWorks LLC, 1992–2003), s.v. "κηρύσσω."

6 κηρύσσων, present active participle, nominative masculine singular from κηρύσσω.

7 *Thayer's Lexicon*, s.v. "κηρύσσω."

8 **William Hendricksen,** *I and II Timothy and Titus* (Grand Rapids: Baker, 1957), 89.

9 "Town crier": "Bells were not the only attention getting device—in Holland, a gong was the instrument of choice for many, and in France they used a drum, or a hunting horn," accessed August 2007 from en.wikipedia.org/wiki/Town_crier.

10 "Proclaim" in Jonah 3:2 is from the exact same Greek work (LXX) that is used in 2 Timothy 4:2.

11 Hendriksen, *I and II Timothy and Titus*, 309.

12 The same root word for "herald" is used in Matthew 4:17 and 4:23.

13 "Town crier," en.wikipedia.org/wiki/Town_crier.

14 Found also in 1 Timothy 5:21 and 2 Timothy 2:14.

15 Daniel Wallace, *Greek Grammar Beyond the Basics: An Exegetical Syntax of the New Testament* (1996, 2003 by BibleWorks LLC), s.v. "Διαμαρτύρομαι." Wallace says this is a "constative aorist, signifying 'a solemn or categorical command.' The stress is not 'begin an action,' nor 'continue to act.' Rather, the stress is on the solemnity and urgency of the action."

16 *BDAG*, s.v. "Διαμαρτύρομαι."

17 Matthew Henry, notes on 2 Timothy 4:1, *Complete Commentary on the Whole Bible*, bible.crosswalk.com/Commentaries/MatthewHenryComplete/mhc-com.cgi?book=2ti&chapter=004.

18 Charles Haddon Spurgeon, accessed August 2007 from www.answers.com/topic/charles-spurgeon.

19 John Calvin on 2 Timothy 4:2, *Commentary on Timothy, Titus, Philemon*, accessed from www.ccel.org/ccel/calvin/calcom43.iv.v.i.html.

20 A.W. Tozer, *Man: The Dwelling Place of God*, accessed August 2007 from www.worldinvisible.com/library/tozer/5j00.0010/5j00.0010.10.htm.

21 Fred B. Craddock, *As One Without Authority* (St Louis: Chalice Press, 2001). Craddock's book title exemplifies the current trend in "conversational" preaching. Inductive preaching of this kind carries little actual authority. Preaching and authority cannot be separated.

22 Albert Mohler, "Expository Preaching and the Recovery of Christian Worship (Part Three)," accessed August 2007 from www.albertmohler.com/commentary_read.php?cdate=2005-08-11.

23 C.H. Spurgeon, from a sermon, 'Harvest men wanted,' preached August 17 1873. Accessed from www.recoverthegospel.com/Old%20Recover%20the%20Gospel%20Site/Spurgeon/Spurgeon%201001-2000/1127.pdf.

24 Charles Haddon Spurgeon, "How to Meet the Evils of the Age," (ch. 4) in *An All-Round Ministry: Addresses to Ministers and Students*, accessed from www.spurgeon.org/misc/aarm04.htm.

25 Quoted by **Eugene P. Harder** of New Hope Community Church, March 19 2000. Accessed from www.newhope.bc.ca/00-03-19.htm.

26 George Whitefield, accessed from thinkexist.com/quotation/ it_is_a_poor_sermon_that_gives_no_offense-that/158297.html.

27 **Martin Luther** to Philip Melanchthon, quoted in **David L. Larsen,** *The Anatomy of Preaching: Identifying the Issues in Preaching Today* (Grand Rapids: Kregel, 1999), 99.

28 **Archbishop Richard Whately,** English prelate and theologian (1787–1863). Accessed from www.giga-sa.com/quotes/authors/richard_whately_a003.

29 Chapter 4 was totally devoted to this idea, but I wanted to list this here because it is listed in 2 Timothy 4:2.

30 **Phillips Brooks,** *Lectures on Preaching: Delivered before the Divinity School of Yale College in January and February 1877* (London: H.R. Allenson, 1877), 129.

31 **John Calvin,** *The Second Epistle of Paul to the Corinthians, and the Epistles to Timothy, Titus and Philemon*, vol. 10, Calvin's New Testament Commentaries, ed. David Torrance and Thomas Torrance (Grand Rapids: Eerdmans, 1964), 335.

32 **Ann Douglas,** *The Feminization of American Culture* (New York: The Noonday Press, 1998).

33 **R.L. Dabney,** *Evangelical Eloquence: A Course of Lectures on Preaching* (Carlisle, PA: Banner of Truth, 1999; originally published as *Sacred Rhetoric*, 1870; first Banner of Truth edition published as *R.L. Dabney on Preaching*, 1979), 36–37.

34 **John Stott,** *The Preacher's Portrait* (London: Billing & Sons, 1961), 37.

Jesus preached discipleship

I was once helping a local church find a potential pastor, yet they had reservations about their number one choice. They were concerned that he was leaving his current church "because there were no other leaders to help me." My question was, "How long was he there?" The answer came back: "Three to four years." I immediately knew that man was not the right candidate, because he, as an elder and leader, was responsible to disciple other leaders. He was the problem in the equation of "no other leadership." He had "made his own bed." Pastors and New Testament leaders must reproduce themselves, while congregations need to be ready to be stretched and taught through discipleship.

This chapter will begin by looking at Christ's broad call to discipleship (the Great Commission in Matthew 28:18–20), then it will tighten the lens by examining Paul's charge for Timothy to disciple other men with the goal of having them teach others (the Great Transmission in 2 Timothy 2:2), and it will finish by providing a practical "teaching template" for leaders to use in actually discipling others to teach (a "what exactly to teach other men" section). The bulk of the chapter will lay out a comprehensive agenda for pastors and elders in discipling others to proclaim God's truth.

Jesus taught the importance of discipleship

MATTHEW 28:18–20 (THE GREAT COMMISSION)

The Gospel of Matthew ends with what is commonly (and rightly) called the "Great Commission." Christ's last words before His ascension contain the marching orders for His disciples and for every disciple of Christ throughout history. He is going to leave the disciples soon, and the timing of these words gives them greater significance and emphasis, or *gravitas*. In three short verses, Jesus summarizes the entire mission of Christianity with a call to "make disciples," saying,

All authority has been given to Me in heaven and on earth. Go therefore and make disciples of all the nations, baptizing them in the name of the Father and the Son and the Holy Spirit, teaching them to observe all that I commanded you; and lo, I am with you always, even to the end of the age (Matthew 28:18–20).

The imperative "make disciples" carries the idea of "to cause one to be a pupil, teach."[1] The apostles were given no choice: they were to make disciples of others. Their students needed to be learners of Christ. Making disciples was accomplished by "going," "baptizing," and "teaching" the pupils.[2] Robert Mounce stresses this kind of discipleship, saying, "Both *baptizontes* and *didaskontes* are participles governed by the imperative *matheteusate*."[3] These modifiers specifically characterize the essence of how to make disciples.

A command like this from Jesus would result in the production of new disciples. Subsequently, these new disciples would also be exhorted to make more disciples. Every new disciple would then be a part of passing on the truths of Jesus Christ to the next generation. D.A. Carson says, "These in turn pass on the truth they received. So a means is provided for successive generations to remain in contact with Jesus' teachings."[4] The cycle must continue from the ascension until the Lord's return.

The clear and explicit call to "make disciples" has been appropriately used by the church to evangelize unbelievers. The importance of evangelism cannot be overstated, but Christ's command is more comprehensive and demands that the church teach both outside and inside her walls. The breadth of this command requires Christ's disciples to engage in more than just the proclamation of Christ's payment for the forgiveness of sins; it also requires instruction about holy living. The entire Christian life must be addressed. Alfred Plummer is insightful when he states, "It is evident from the threefold charge that the teaching which suffices for discipleship and for admission to Christian communion is not all that is requisite. After baptism much additional instruction will be required, especially for Gentiles, who knew nothing about the teaching of the O.T., either as regards doctrine or morality."[5] This charge compels and obliges the one discipling to teach everything from salvation to glorification.

While Luke's account of the Great Commission (Luke 24:46–49) seems to focus solely on the necessity of evangelism, Matthew 28:18–20 allows a more comprehensive scope of what disciples should be taught.[6] Since Jesus said in Matthew 28:20, "teaching them to observe all that I commanded you," then Christ's current disciples needed to teach the next generation of disciples "to observe" everything that Jesus taught, and they needed to teach subsequent generations everything.[7] The only difference would be that the original "eyewitnesses" would fade away and there would then only be "ear-witnesses" to what the Lord said or did.[8]

Jesus wanted to ensure that His disciples passed on all of His teachings.[9] The point is simply that every command that Jesus gave to the disciples must be taught to others. Matthew's own penning of the first Gospel is, in a sense, direct obedience to the command of Jesus Christ, because Matthew himself is teaching others all the commands of Christ as he records the Messiah's words in his Gospel.

Matthew 28:18–20 establishes the general idea of discipleship which envelops evangelism and every other component of Christianity. Certainly, pastors are not exempt from this command, a command that follows Christ's example of intimate disciple-making.

Jesus' apostles taught the importance of discipling others to teach

2 TIMOTHY 2:2 (THE GREAT TRANSMISSION)

The Apostle Paul, even though he was an apostle who was "untimely born" (1 Corinthians 15:8), received the "discipleship marching orders" from Jesus, and he obeyed them. Jesus gave the call for discipleship in a general way, but now the Spirit of Christ directs Paul to be more specific about discipleship in his second letter to Timothy.

Paul, by now an aging apostle, is wrapping up his ministry, and he writes to Timothy, his beloved son in the faith. In no time at all, Paul will meet his Savior face to face, so he relays the last bit of urgent and vital information to Timothy from his prison cell in Rome. Paul explicitly and plainly exhorts Timothy, and every future church leader, to be faithful in the task of reproducing himself through discipleship. Paul directly urges and presses Timothy to disciple others, saying,

The things which you have heard from me in the presence of many witnesses, entrust these to faithful men who will be able to teach others also (2 Timothy 2:2).

Paul charges his young protégé to be faithful to train other men in the same way Paul himself trained Timothy (and possibly the same way Jesus trained Paul personally through an extraordinary revelation—Galatians 1:12).

Contextually, the command is delivered immediately after challenging Timothy to "be strong in the grace that is in Christ Jesus" (2 Timothy 2:1). Paul's command to disciple must be carried out in the strength which God alone supplies by grace. Furthermore, in 2 Timothy 1:13 Paul commanded Timothy to "retain the standard of sound words which [he had] heard from [Paul], in the faith and love which are in Christ Jesus." Paul was calling for Timothy to hold the gospel safely (the *Friberg Lexicon* describes the verb translated "retain" as "retain something safely—keep, preserve"[10]). The present active imperative of ἔχω highlights the determination which Timothy (and all pastors and elders after him) should possess in holding the Word in security and safekeeping.

However, in 2:2, Timothy needs to do more than simply guard the gospel trust. The word translated "entrust" means to commit, or to put before someone. Some say it carries the idea of "to entrust for safekeeping, give over, entrust, commend … for safekeeping or transmission to others."[11] As a part of faithfully protecting his stewardship, Timothy needs to train others in the ministry so that they can successfully educate others with the truth. Gordon D. Fee explains the relation to 1:13 with these words: "The first task he is to be strengthened for is tied closely to the imperatives of 1:13–14. Just as Timothy must 'keep safe what has been entrusted to him,' so also he is now to entrust (the verb form of the noun 'deposit' in 1:14; cf. 1 Tim. 6:20) them to reliable men who, in turn, will also be qualified to teach others."[12] The safekeeping of the gospel is partially achieved in 2:2 by successfully teaching it to others.

Paul is not explicitly telling Timothy to create more elders by discipleship. Instead, the objective for Timothy is simply to teach and train others. A. T. Hanson affirms this objective, saying, "We certainly have here a doctrine of succession, but it is succession in teaching rather than succession in authorized office."[13] Teaching is essential to the well-being of the Christian faith, and it is mandatory for the local church if she desires to function biblically. Even though George W. Knight III argues that "Plummer is correct in suggesting that this brief reference to men being taught so that they can teach others gives evidence of 'the earliest traces of a theological school,'"[14] it does not mean that this only reveals some type of formal school. Again, Paul did not specify that Timothy should train up elders, deacons, or even other pastors; rather, he gave a very generic and general charge to train those who would teach. Paul did not explicitly exclude laymen; rather, the language here suggests that they should be included.

This charge shows the three levels of discipleship,[15] but the nature of discipleship needs to be further discussed. Seldom does one hear about the exact features of this commanded discipleship. Paul surely taught Timothy more than just the facts when it came to theology; he surely taught him how to handle the Old Testament, how to interpret it, and, among other things, how to teach it. William Hendricksen proposes that Paul is conveying this idea: "Let Timothy be a teacher. Even more, let him produce teachers! Timothy needs this experience, and what is far more important, the church needs the teachers!"[16] Pastors should disciple men so that they might be better husbands, serve the body of Christ more, and be ambassadors in the workplace, but pastors also need to include the training of laymen to be Bible teachers.

From the negative perspective, the entrusting "consists in their not losing, neglecting, ignoring, or falsifying (as will the false teachers mentioned in this letter) what Paul has said, and positively consists of their 'handling accurately the word of truth' (2:15)."[17] The vital, life-giving information must be handed on with as much determination and care as an Olympian would transfer a baton in a relay race. Timothy will one day leave or die (like all pastors and church leaders) and knowing that fact, he must train other leaders and laymen to understand sound doctrine well enough to continue to pass it along by teaching. Church leaders today must train others to effectively understand and teach the Word of God. Those in leadership of the local church must disciple others and prepare them to teach the next generation. The "Great Transmission" of truth will lead to a healthy and mature church.

Speaking of the maturation of the body, Ephesians 4:11–13 is another passage that, although very generic, presupposes teaching discipleship. Paul stresses God's desire for the maturation of His church and the means to that growth, saying,

And He gave some as apostles, and some as prophets, and some as evangelists, and some as pastors and teachers, for the equipping of the saints for the work of service, to the building up of the body of Christ; until we all attain to the unity of the faith, and of the knowledge of the Son of God, to a mature man, to the measure of the stature which belongs to the fullness of Christ (Ephesians 4:11–13).

The pastor-teachers[18] assist the body of Christ by equipping those under their care to accomplish the work of the ministry in the church. Friberg states that the word translated "equip" means "a process of adjustment that results in a complete preparedness, equipping, perfecting, making adequate."[19] The equipping has the goal of making the body of Christ sufficient and completely qualified for her task of every type of ministry.[20] Just as a broken bone needs setting so that proper healing can take place, so the pastor-teacher must properly align the theological bone structure of the sheep so that God may use them for ministry.[21]

The body is "built up" and so constructed that, through the power of the Holy Spirit, it will be made sufficient for all that Christ calls it to be. "The purpose of Christ's bestowing these gifts on the church is expressed in the three successive prepositional phrases … 'for the equipment of the saints', 'for the work of ministry', and 'for building the body of Christ.'"[22] The saints are the ones who really get the ministry done. The significance is highlighted when one recalls the One who actually gives the gifts to the church, namely, Jesus Christ. The stress in the original Greek is not principally upon the gifts, but upon the Lord Jesus who gave them.[23] The whole focus is upon the Head of the church and how He Himself desires a fully functioning body and toward that end gives gifts to the local church.

The local church leadership must prove to be good stewards of God's people and train them in all areas. Discussing the goal of ministry, Harold W. Hoehner says, "Here the preposition εισ introduces the goal of these gifted people, namely, to prepare other saints for the work of the ministry."[24] Pastor-teachers must equip the saints to do the work of the ministry. Certainly "the work of the ministry" must include teaching, and because ministry is the goal, teaching must be included in the equipping of the saints.

Paul used very general terms so that the teaching and discipleship would include the propagation of both speaking and non-speaking ministries. Nothing in the text limits the church and her leadership to training people only for deacon-like duties that exclude teaching. This general statement of ministry necessitates the training of men to teach the Christian faith. Even laymen are required to know and understand the Word of God so that they might evangelize, train others, and instruct their own families. What would limit Timothy from pouring himself into other leaders and laymen who would be able to teach? The aim of equipping in Ephesians 4:12 is "for the work of service." Surely there would be some in the congregation whom God had endowed with the spiritual gift of teaching, so the pastor would need to help those men to use their gifts to the glory of God. Incorporated into pastoral ministry is teaching others for the purpose of having them teach what they have learned. Pastors must disciple and train others for the work of Christ's ministry, and this discipleship includes teaching others to teach and preach well.

Application for preachers, elders, leaders, and Bible teachers

EMPHASIZE THE IMPORTANCE OF DISCIPLING
CHURCH MEMBERS TO TEACH THE BIBLE

Many conceive of discipleship as teaching the disciples to be punctual, to have their "quiet times," to be godly spouses, and to work at their jobs with an eye toward heaven. These are great and admirable tasks every new Christian needs help with understanding and implementing. But is that all there is to teach them? What about the Great Transmission? How does a leader in the church actually teach disciples to teach the Bible? What is it necessary to teach them? I submit that there are three overarching topics that must be taught to everyone who wants to accurately teach the Bible: rules for interpretation of the Bible; exegesis; and homiletical skills. Each of these three topics can be taught for one month to three months. Each topic builds upon the prior subject, so order is important. These topics will help the local church to raise up more leaders who can transmit God's truth through teaching. The leaderless church, like the church of the man I discussed at the beginning of this chapter, need not exist if you follow this template.

Are you a church leader who is committed to discipleship? Have you excluded discipling others so that they might become teachers of the Bible? People more adept at teaching the Bible are better evangelists and "family worship" leaders and will excel in their daily devotions.

Who would argue that the church needs more godly teachers who are skilled in the Word! But who is going to train them? It is the current church's leadership that has been given the mantle to train leaders. Every leader begins as a layman. Pastors need to disciple laymen in all areas, especially in Bible teaching. A. Boyd Luter's diagnosis of the diminishing numbers of proficient church teachers is astute. He says, "Certainly discipling should be a source for producing capable teachers (2 Timothy 2:2). If the responsibility for helping believers to mature in order to be able to teach (Hebrews 5:11–14) were taken more seriously, perhaps the problem of teacher shortages in a large number of churches today would be solved."[25] In light of this statement, I propose to lay the groundwork for pastors to instruct laymen to teach the Bible.

A paradigm for pastors to disciple laymen to teach[26]

The remaining part of this chapter provides a simple exemplar for leaders to train men to excel as teachers of God's Holy Word. It lays out, in three main sections, the basic elements of instruction for teachers as they reach toward the goal of teaching the Bible accurately. Due to time and scope, it is only a primer by design and should be used as a platform for more detailed instruction and discipleship. Its objective is to have you understand how to specifically train laymen to understand the Bible better with the goal of teaching it. I want to give you a starting point, although you may certainly cut and paste it as you please. Springboarding from someone else's idea is easier than starting from scratch. The following should be taught over a minimum of a three-month time frame.

A few comments before the actual template is given: in order to teach others, one must first properly understand the subject. It sounds absurd to state anything else, but many today deny this tenet by practicing the very opposite. Contrary to current thinking, spirituality does not abandon the hard work of trying to understand what God specifically articulated in His Word. Walter Kaiser, a modern pioneer in biblical preaching, declares,

Let it be stated as a sort of first principle that preparation for preaching is always a movement which must begin with the text of Scripture and have as its goal the proclamation of that Word in such a way that it can be heard with all its poignancy and relevancy to the modern situation without dismissing one iota of its original normativeness.[27]

Can such a task be accomplished without the preliminary toil of proper interpretation? The Word must be rightly divided before it can be accurately taught.

The *telos*, or goal, of teaching must be arrived at by the means of fitting hermeneutics and exegesis. How can teaching the text be divorced from the understanding of it? Are these not inexorably linked? Is it possible to pass on what one has not grasped? Jerry Vines and David Allen state the obvious by declaring, "Hermeneutics, exegesis, and proclamation form the crucial triad with which every pastor must reckon. A proper biblical hermeneutic provides the philosophical underpinnings which undergird the exegetical task. Likewise, a proper exegetical methodology provides the foundation for the sermon. Then, of course, proper sermon delivery is necessary to carry home God's truth to the hearer."[28] The obligation is on the church leadership to train those in the church who wish to learn the methodology requisite to understand the Bible so that they will interpret it in a way in which they will arrive at the meaning God intended. It accomplishes nothing if the teacher and the student do not understand what they are studying. No benefit is achieved in misunderstanding God's Word and then teaching that misunderstanding to others. On the contrary, great damage can be done to the local body.

How can this error be avoided? It must begin with a binding commitment to both an accurate hermeneutical process and a precise exegetical method, and then proceed to the actual teaching. Let's look at the first section in the paradigm.

1. TRAIN YOUR DISCIPLES TO APPROACH THE BIBLE WITH A SYSTEM OF RULES FOR INTERPRETATION

The system of rules for Bible interpretation is commonly called "hermeneutics." Scholars further define it by saying,

Hermeneutics … is both a science and an art. As a science, it enunciates principles, investigates the laws of thought and language, and classifies its facts and results. As an art, it teaches what application these principles should have, and establishes their soundness by showing their practical value in the elucidation of the more difficult Scriptures. The hermeneutical art thus cultivates and establishes a valid exegetical procedure.[29]

Church leaders should be under compulsion to introduce their laymen to this fundamental concept. It could be said that everyone who studies the Bible uses a hermeneutic. However, a system of interpretation that is unbiblical and fails to honor God must be avoided at all cost.

If the teacher has a goal to properly honor God in his teaching, he will need help. My goal is to set forth several nonnegotiables with regard to teaching laymen about hermeneutics. Granted, this training will be taught at the most basic level, but even the hardest concepts can be put within the reach of any literate layman.

1.1 DISCIPLES MUST BE TAUGHT TO SEE UNDERSTANDING AUTHORIAL INTENT AS THEIR GOAL

Assuming that the starting point is valid (that the Bible can be understood), one must find out exactly what the human author meant when God's Spirit inspired him to write. Without definitive meanings, the students would be working within a morass of subjectivity; anyone's interpretation of a given passage would be just as valid as everyone else's. Thankfully, "traditional hermeneutics assumed that a text contained a determinate meaning which with the proper exegetical method could be discerned by an interpreter."[30] Because of this principle, students should be taught that determining authorial intent is neither optional nor discretionary; rather, this principle is the very essence of their work. Without determining the intent, they cannot proceed.

The heart of biblical hermeneutics is to uncover and reveal what the biblical author wanted to convey. Kaiser concurs, saying, "Hermeneutics may be regarded as the theory that guides exegesis; exegesis may be understood ... to be the practice of and the set of procedures for discovering the author's intended meaning."[31] All students need to be thoroughly steeped in this concept because it will affect the way they preach and what they teach.

"The opposite of exposition is 'imposition.'"[32] The latest, most dangerous trend in imposition is known as the "reader-response theory." It puts a majority of the stress on what the interpreter thinks the text means to him, not what it meant to the author when he originally wrote it. Kaiser documents the entrance of this type of fallacious thinking, stating,

In my judgment, the most dramatic moment in the entire twentieth century came in 1946 when E.K. Wimsatt and Monroe Beardsley published their article "The Intentional Fallacy" in the *Swanee Review* ... which [is] now understood to advocate something like this: Whatever an author may have meant or intended to say by his or her written words is now irrelevant to the meanings we have come to assign as the meaning we see in that author's text![33]

Sandra M. Schneiders also summarizes this type of philosophy as she critiques it:

The text becomes ... semantically independent of the intention of its author. It now means whatever it means, and all that it can mean, regardless of whether or not the author intended that meaning. Indeed ... the intention of the author is no longer available to us in any case. Furthermore ... it is of the very nature of truly great texts to be characterized by a certain excess of meaning that could not have been part of the intention of the author.[34]

The right question is, "What did the author mean when he said …?" and not, "What does this passage me to me?" Students should be taught to ask with Kaiser, "If individual speakers or writers are not sovereign over the use of their own words, and if meaning is not a return to how they intended their own words to be regarded, then we are in a most difficult situation."[35] Sadly, this is the type of study that is rife within the undiscerning circles of Bible teachers today. A crucial step in hermeneutics must be acceptance of the truism, "Surely the meaning resides in what the author intended by the passage as opposed to what the readers may take it to mean to them."[36]

1.2 DISCIPLES MUST BE INSTRUCTED TO SEEK
TO DETERMINE THE SINGLE MEANING OF THE TEXT

Since the goal of hermeneutics is acquiring the author's intended meaning, expository students must be taught that the meaning of any given passage is singular. God has the ability to communicate to humans through His Word (revelation) and God has chosen to communicate with words and sentences. These words then give a meaning that is static and fixed. If the text means solely what the author intended, then by definition it must be singular. Dual intention would be expressed plainly by the author. This understanding reinforces the logical consequence that the meaning is found in the text of Scripture and not in the reader. The passage itself contains the meaning, and that meaning is singular.

Practically, the problem can arise when the student does not understand that meaning and applications often overlap. Wisdom remembers the axiom, "Interpretation is one; application is many."[37] Kaiser rightly discusses the difference between the "meaning" of the original text and the "significance" for the modern day.[38] The goal should be to uncover the sole meaning of the text and leave application for post-exegetical study.

1.3 DISCIPLES MUST BE INSTRUCTED TO USE THE
GRAMMATICAL-HISTORICAL APPROACH OF HERMENEUTICS

Expository students should be taught the basics of hermeneutics, especially how the Bible is to be read and interpreted "literally." The literal concept can often be pushed to the extreme, so much so that it can ignore literary devices and is thus marginalized as a wooden hermeneutic.

Introducing students to a primer on grammatical-historical interpretation is wise and can alleviate any misunderstanding.

"To interpret 'literally' means to explain the original sense of the speaker or writer according to the normal, customary and proper usages of words and language."[39] Alternatively, it could also be called the "grammatical-historical" manner of hermeneutics, because the meaning of each word, phrase, and sentence is determined by grammatical and historical factors and considerations. Said another way, "The aim of grammatico-historical method is to determine the sense required by the laws of grammar and the facts of history."[40]

To elaborate, students should comprehend that application of "grammatical" hermeneutical principles will yield a meaning found within the confines of regular language and its usage. The "historical" aspect of this method will affirm that the meaning discovered in the text is influenced by the period of history during which the text was written. Viable alternatives are nonexistent. Without this method, the search for objectivity is seriously compromised. What logical or rational check would there be on the variety of man's creative interpretations? Charles C. Ryrie understands the logic behind this method of interpretation as he bluntly says,

The purpose of language itself seems to require literal interpretation. Language was given by God for the purpose of being able to communicate with mankind … If God is the originator of language and if the chief purpose of originating it was to convey His message to humanity, then it must follow that He, being all-wise and all-loving, originated sufficient language to convey all that was in His heart to tell mankind. Furthermore, it must also follow that He would use language and expect people to understand it in its literal, normal and plain sense.[41]

The background to this style of interpretation is enlightening:

The term "grammatical-historical interpretation" was used originally by Karl A.B. Keil. The term "grammatical," however, is somewhat misleading in our ears today, for normally we mean the arrangement of words and the construction of sentences. But Keil did not have this meaning in mind when he used the term. Instead, he had in mind the Greek word *gramma*, which approximates what we would mean by the term "literal" (to use a synonym derived from Latin). Keil's grammatical sense was what we would call the simple, direct, plain, ordinary, natural, or literal sense of the phrases, clauses, and sentences. Keil's use of "historical" meant that the interpreter had to consider these words in relation to the time, circumstances, events, and persons in that historical period in which the author wrote. Thus, the grand object for Keil was, as it is for us, to ascertain the *usus loquendi*, that is, the specific use of the words, as they were employed by the writer under consideration and/or as prevalent in the day and age in which he wrote.[42]

So, whether "grammatical" refers to the literal understanding or the grammar behind the understanding, the result is the same: the text must speak for itself, as God has superintended the author to write in order to convey His thoughts to mankind.

1.4 DISCIPLES MUST BE EDUCATED ABOUT THE PLACE OF "PRE-UNDERSTANDING"

As students strive for objectivity in Bible interpretation, they must be taught to be aware of the theological "baggage" that they themselves bring into the process of interpretation. They should pursue the meaning of the text with the goal of being objective while at the same time recognizing that their own backgrounds (social, cultural, theological, and personal) can influence their interpretations. Influence or pre-understanding has no place in a hermeneutical system that has the purpose of bringing the teacher to understand the author's intention alone. "Grammatical-historical" interpretation could easily turn into "grammatical-historical-theological" interpretation, and it would then undermine and erode the search for the author's meaning.

Carson wryly quips, "Carl F.H. Henry is fond of saying that there are two kinds of presuppositionalists: those who admit it and those who don't."[43] The point here is that pre-understanding is inevitable, but it should be consciously wrestled with and then suppressed. Inevitably, a person's background, makeup, and life experiences will affect his interpretation, but pre-understanding should be stifled and curbed until the last possible moment. How does pre-understanding flesh itself out? The key is to make sure that theological presuppositions are dealt with only at the end of the hermeneutical process. Robert Thomas is cognizant of the latent pre-understanding in everyone, but he prudently suggests that presuppositions must be faced at the end of the process of determining meaning, and not at the beginning. He says, "By bringing pre-understanding to bear on interpretation at the outset of the process, interpreters are starting with contemporary considerations rather than those connected with the initial setting of a passage."[44]

2. TRAIN YOUR DISCIPLES IN EXEGESIS

Exegesis is simply "An implementation of valid interpretive principles."[45] Exegesis puts into practice the very principles of grammatical-historical hermeneutics. It actually does the work of determining what God said and what He meant when He said it. "The purpose of exegesis is to 'lead out' the meaning which has been deposited in the biblical text by the writer. Exegesis is of crucial importance because it is the foundation for theology and preaching. We cannot communicate the meaning of God's word via preaching until we have understood it ourselves."[46] The expository student must, then, be taught the very basics of exegesis to guarantee the right interpretation of the passage so that he might teach the Bible with fidelity.

2.1 DISCIPLES MUST BE SHOWN HOW TO ANALYZE A TEXT EXEGETICALLY

If the goal of exegesis is to implement proper hermeneutical principles in order to find out what the biblical author intended, then the student should be taught specifically how to investigate Bible passages with meticulous scrutiny. God's propositional truth must be probed within "its syntactical, lexical, literary, historical, social/cultural, geographical, and theological contexts."[47]

Exegesis can best be carried out by asking questions and observing a passage with microscopic detail. This observation assumes that the passage has been read many times and that the student is quite familiar with it. The best place to begin is by asking questions in an overview fashion. For example, these questions would include factors of theme and the purpose of the book, the local and far contexts, key words and verbs, grammar, word order, and the relationship of the words to the sentence and theme of the book. Moving toward a more analytical assessment, questions then include those of recurring words and thoughts, contrasts, comparisons, summary verses, and the progression of thinking in the mind of the author. Lastly, the generic "who," "what," "when," "where," "how," and "why" questions asked of the passage should be asked regarding the cultural, historical, geographical, and Eastern influences. These help the reader appreciate the passage at hand.

Students should be instructed to analyze every detail of the passages that they are studying. This analysis can be facilitated by the use of a theological library. Bible translations and the use of other tools, such as commentaries (exegetical, homiletical, and devotional), atlases, and lexicons must be discussed. Special caution is urged against improper word studies and "illegitimate totality transfers."[48] While laymen may not be able to understand the case functions of nouns or the tense, voice, person, mood, and number of verbs, they will become familiar with how commentaries deal with issues of grammar and how they affect the meaning of a verse.

2.2 DISCIPLES MUST BE TRAINED IN DETERMINING THE ROLE OF "ANALOGY OF THE FAITH"

What is the "analogy of the faith"? Essentially, it teaches that Scripture interprets other Scripture. When a passage is difficult to understand, the rest of the Bible is to be consulted. In many ways, the analogy of the faith is the acceptance of systematic theology into hermeneutics. Systematic theology can be very helpful, but it should not be "front-loaded" in the process of interpretation. The text must say what it says, and not what other texts make it say. Certainly God's mind is one, and the Bible does not contradict itself, but one must be careful of using the analogy of the faith in a default manner while interpreting difficult passages. The place of its use is correctly described by Thomas, who says, "The analogy of faith finds its proper use at the conclusion of the exegetical process as a double check on the accuracy of exegesis rather than at the beginning of the process as a pre-understanding that will adversely affect the accuracy of the exegesis."[49] The analogy of the faith should be used for a check or benchmark that is used at the end of the process of interpretation rather than as a tool that should be consulted early in the process of exegesis.

The best way to help teach students the pitfalls of this device is to clearly show that the analogy of faith has a historical backdrop and should be utilized carefully. Kaiser teaches,

The Reformers courageously argued that all faith and practice must be based on Scripture alone (*sola Scriptura*). But the Scriptures still had to be interpreted. The Reformers' solution was to announce that "Scripture interprets Scripture" (*Scriptura Scripturam interpretatur*). The analogy of faith became a corollary of "Scripture interprets Scripture" … Many have forgotten that *analogia fidei* as used by the Reformers was a *relative* expression especially aimed at the tyrannical demands of tradition.[50]

In other words, the fight against tradition pushed this device to the forefront, and it should be used today with caution as we are in a different historical situation altogether.

2.3 DISCIPLES MUST BE TUTORED IN THE ROLE OF THE HOLY SPIRIT IN BIBLE STUDY
Students must remember that the Bible is more than a human production and that God Himself is the primary Author. Students need the Holy Spirit's illumination in their task of exegesis. Unbelievers can understand the grammar of a passage, yet they are in the dark with respect to its meaning since they do not have the Holy Spirit. Just as the Spirit guided the apostles into truth (John 16:13), so He now illumines the minds of believers as they study the ancient text or modern translation. A believer's thoughts about a passage do not guarantee an infallible interpretation; no true interpretation can be made apart from the Holy Spirit. Additionally, it should be taught that "the work of the Spirit in interpretation does not mean that He gives some interpreters a 'hidden' meaning divergent from the normal, literal meaning of the passage."[51]

Teaching students the role of the Holy Spirit will remind them of the gravity of recognizing the Spirit's role in Bible study. Art Azurdia frankly states, "I believe that the greatest impediment to the advancement of the gospel in our time is the attempt of the church of Jesus Christ to do the work of God apart from the truth and the power of the Spirit of God."[52] Happily, God's mandate to rightly divide the Word also comes with His gracious provision of the Holy Spirit.

The recognition of the Holy Spirit should manifest itself in the life of the student in his increased desire to pray and his dependence upon the Lord and His illumination. The student's prayer should be for understanding, faithful interpretation, a changed life based on the calls in the text for holiness, the proper public teaching of the Word, and for the listeners to have "ears to hear" what the Spirit is saying through His Word. What Charles Bridges said of the preacher is true for every Bible teacher, including laymen: "Without prayer, a Minister is of no use to the church, nor of any advantage to mankind. He sows; and God gives no increase. He preaches; and his words are only like 'sounding brass, or a tinkling cymbal.'"[53]

SUMMARY

Sidney Greidanus aptly summarizes the need for all Bible teachers, including laymen, to understand hermeneutics and exegesis, saying,

At heart, expository preaching is not just a method but a commitment, a view of the essence of preaching, a homiletical approach to preach the Scriptures. This underlying commitment, in turn, is bound to reveal itself in a method in which preachers tie themselves to the Scriptures and, as heralds of Christ, seek to proclaim only that which the Scriptures proclaim.[54]

Laymen must be taught the fundamentals of the hermeneutical philosophy and exegesis because they too will be subjected to the "stricter judgment" of James 3:1.

3. TRAIN YOUR DISCIPLES IN SOME HOMILETICAL SKILLS

All the study and preparation come to a climax when the students actually articulate the fruit of their exegesis and study. What must leaders in the local church teach their laymen when it comes to the actual proclamation of the Bible (in whatever setting it might occur)? In a nonexhaustive fashion I wish to elucidate several key points that must be taught to faithful laymen. There could be much more to teach, but these basic elements lay the foundation for accurate and God-honoring teaching. Even pastors overlook many building blocks, so their importance must not be taken for granted.

After the exegetical sweat and toil is completed, the student is then allowed to move on to the actual proclamation of the text. The order is critical, because the application must flow from exegesis. Sinclair Ferguson agrees, saying, "Exegetical preaching, therefore, sees as its fundamental task the explanation of the text in its context, the unfolding of its principles, and only then their application to the world of the hearers."[55]

3.1 DISCIPLES MUST BE INSTRUCTED THAT THE POINT OF THE SERMON MUST BE THE POINT OF THE TEXT

The goal of every Bible teacher should be faithfulness to the text of Scripture. Students must reflect the thoughts of God whether they endeavor to teach their families, the children in the nursery, or the church youth group. Since the exegetical process seeks to determine the meaning of the author, this meaning must be communicated to the listener. Sadly, this conclusion is not reached by all independently, so students must be reinforced with this directive. The teacher should never use his platform (or pulpit) to drive his own agenda; rather, he speaks in the place of God or on His behalf. Ramesh Richard echoes this sentiment when giving a simple definition of exposition: "Basically, expository preaching helps the preacher promote God's agenda for his people."[56] God's agenda, found in His revelation, must stem from the Word itself. The ball of exposition must be tethered to the text.

Miller Maclure verbalizes the Puritans' connection between the text and teaching it: "For the Puritans, the sermon is not just hinged to Scripture; it quite literally exists inside the Word of God; the text is not in the sermon, but the sermon is in the text."[57] The danger lies in the quicksand of imposing the teacher's ideas onto the text of Scripture instead of exposing God's mind (imposition versus exposition). Exegesis, as stated earlier, is critical to the process of teaching, so it must not be switched to eisegesis as the message of God is actually delivered.

This connection between the text and the sermon demonstrates the nexus of faithfulness to the God of the Word. The point of the passage of Scripture must translate into the main point of the message proclaimed. Said in a more exhaustive way, "The task of interpreters of the Bible is to find out the meaning of a statement (command, question) for the author and for the first hearers or readers, and thereupon to transmit that meaning to modern readers."[58] The Bible is called "revelation" for a reason, and that is because it discloses God's own personal thoughts. It divulges the very mind of God, and therefore all students must be determined to let God speak by crafting a message that does not stifle or muzzle the Word of God.

What must be avoided at all costs is taking the Bible and simply using it as a jumping-off point for a personal agenda of the teacher. Even if the personal agenda is biblically correct (as opposed to textually correct), this kind of teaching must be shunned so that all the listeners will be able to clearly see that the point of the message comes directly from the text. The connection should be clear. Haddon Robinson insightfully asks, "'Does the preacher subject his thought to the Scriptures, or does he subject the Scriptures to his thought?' Is the passage used like the national anthem at a football game—it gets things started but then is not heard again? Or is the text the essence of the sermon to be exposed to the people?"[59]

Sensus plenior is potentially dangerous, and students should be warned about this device. It is defined as "that additional, deeper meaning, intended by God, but not clearly intended by the human author, which is seen to exist in the words of the Biblical text ... when they are studied in the light of further revelation or development in the understanding of revelation."[60] Following the logic of this definition of *sensus plenior*, the point of the sermon could lie beyond the author's original intention. This deeper meaning idea is fraught with landmines of every sort. Safer footing is found by crafting a message that mirrors the implication found in the text. Expository teaching is characterized by allowing "the biblical text to supply both the shape and the content of the message or lesson from that text itself."[61] The point of the passage must be the point of the lesson or message, and the point of the message must be the point of the passage.

3.2. DISCIPLES MUST UNDERSTAND THE CENTRAL THEME OR MAIN PROPOSITION OF THE TEXT

Now the movement is from general to specific. As just stated, the author's intention must trump all other ideas of the text, but the student must also look for the central theme or main proposition surrounding the text itself.

The biblical author has a purpose to convey, and students should hone in on the "big idea"[62] or central thesis of the passage. Students should be taught to ascertain the main argument of the passage or pericope as revealed by the author. The proposition is what the teacher "proposes" to amplify as he teaches. It is one sentence that reveals the purpose and objective of the message and is then expanded during the course of the lesson.

Conceptually, the teacher must be able to distill the passage into its bare essence. This exercise facilitates his thorough comprehension of his material. It assists him with his outline and directed application. J.H. Jowett underlines the importance of the proposition when he says, "I have a conviction that no sermon is ready for preaching, not ready for writing out, until we can express its theme in a short, pregnant sentence as clear as crystal."[63] Every student, when asked, should be able to furnish a one-sentence summary of the passage he has studied. He is not ready to teach it until this goal is achieved.

Understanding the proposition helps more than the teacher. It assists the listeners' comprehension and encourages them to remember the central theme. The benefit of a memory aid is expounded by Charles Simeon: "Reduce your text to a simple proposition ... Screw the word into the minds of your hearers."[64]

The central aim then becomes the springboard for the entire message, including the application. Robinson also connects these by saying, "A sermon should be a bullet, not buckshot. Ideally each sermon is the explanation, interpretation, or application of a single dominant idea supported by other ideas, all drawn from one passage or several passages of Scripture."[65]

The proposition both directs the audience to the theme and limits the extent and direction of the message. Students should be taught that the proposition is very flexible. It can be conveyed in the form of an imperative, indicative, question, or exclamation. It should be clear and concise and is often stated with a plural noun (e.g., "four nonnegotiables"). Once again, this plural noun is important because it gives direction and purpose to the message. MacArthur pushes the homiletical proposition's importance, declaring that it "has a single theme that is crystal clear so that your people know exactly what you are saying, how you have supported it, and how it is applied to their lives. The thing that kills people in what is sometimes called expository preaching is randomly meandering through a passage."[66]

To reiterate, the main point of the passage is put into a plural, propositional form and then all the propositions support the overarching purpose or theme of the message. The students should be taught that the message is crafted around the propositional statement. The proposition may differ slightly from the central idea of the text because two different audiences exist (the original and the modern). No Bible message should go without the homiletical proposition because it ties everything together and gives aim and clarity to the passage at hand.

3.3 DISCIPLES MUST BE COACHED IN HOW TO "BRIDGE"
THE BIBLE PASSAGE TO MODERN LISTENERS BY "PRINCIPLIZATION"

True Bible teaching recognizes the differences in audience, that is, those in the Bible and those today. One can most effectively manage the difference by trying to extract principles from the ancient text and then proclaiming those to the modern-day audience. This approach retains the original meaning and setting while still exhorting the contemporary congregation with the authorial intention of the passage. Kaiser agrees with the "principlizing" approach, saying, "To begin with, let it be stated as a sort of first principle that preparation for preaching is always a movement which must begin with the text of Scripture and have as its goal the proclamation of that Word in such a way that it can be heard with all its poignancy and relevancy to the modern situation without dismissing one iota of its original normativeness."[67]

Some types of Scripture are more easily preached than others. Obviously, the bridges will be fewer in the New Testament epistles and greater in Old Testament Mosaic Law.[68] Students should be coached to ask questions about setting, occasion, purpose, original audience, and cultural ramifications that could limit modern-day application. Henry A. Virkler recognizes the proper amount of caution that is necessary when he says, "Since a behavior in one culture may have a different meaning in another culture, it may be necessary to change the behavioral expression of a scriptural command in order to translate the principle behind that command from one culture and time to another."[69]

The sermon or lesson must be related specifically to the modern hearer. The use of principles helps the student take the Bible, "which was given in a particular time and place and situation, and apply it to people in the modern world who live in another time, another place, and a very different situation."[70]

3.4 DISCIPLES MUST MAKE CERTAIN THAT THE APPLICATION OF THE MESSAGE STEMS FROM THE MEANING OF THE TEXT

A biblical message must include application. God's revelation always demands a response, and in the context of public proclamation, application must be given. One preacher said, "The application of an expository sermon is not complete until the pastor has disclosed the grace in the text that rightly stimulates the obedient response of believers."[71] Many think that exposition is just a huge data dump that only informs the mind and never challenges the soul. But exposition must include how God's revelation should dictate the terms of a life that, by the grace of God, either thinks differently or acts more in accordance with the Word of God.

Care is needed with this potential stumbling block because many simply breeze right into application without regard for biblical accuracy. Robinson poignantly states, "More heresy is preached in application than in Bible exegesis."[72] On its face, this statement is shocking. However, upon further consideration, it becomes a truism: the further one wanders from the inspired text, the more likely one is to teach contrary to it. Students should be trained so that they can be wary of any pitfalls and be proactive in making biblically based applications. To do otherwise would be to truncate the author's intention, and the teacher would therefore fail in his duty to accurately communicate the one and only meaning of his chosen passage. Put bluntly, "We do wrong when we take a text and read our message into it."[73]

Multiple applications from a single text are not the issue here. The Holy Spirit can apply the truth to many situations in many different ways. "We may readily admit that the Scriptures are capable of manifold practical applications."[74] The real important matter deals with the application's origin: it must come straight from the text in an unobscured manner. With lots of options, the students must settle only for the biblical ones when application is taught.

In summary fashion, Hershael W. York and Scott A. Blue declare,

Application in the expository sermon is the process whereby the expositor takes a biblical truth of the text and applies it to the lives of his audience, proclaiming why it is relevant for their lives, practically showing how it should affect their lives, and passionately encouraging them to make necessary changes in their lives in a manner congruent with the original intent of the author.[75]

Notice the phrase "why it is relevant." The authors did not say, "Make it relevant," because the Eternal God of the universe always yields relevant information. The listeners need assistance from the teacher as they strive to understand God's Word and how it relates to them in the form of examples (good or bad), commands, promises, or simply the proper way to think about God. In other words, "Application may be content oriented, relating to what the hearers should believe or value, or it may be conduct oriented, relating to what they should do or obey."[76]

3.5 DISCIPLES MUST BE TAUGHT TO PASSIONATELY EXHORT LISTENERS TO BELIEVE AND OBEY THE LORD

Because "biblical preaching occurs when listeners are enabled to see how their world, like the biblical world, is addressed by the Word of God and are enabled to respond to that Word,"[77] it makes far more sense for application to be given throughout the message instead of pushing it all to the end. Too many Bible teachers wait until the very end of their message and simply "tack on" several points of application as "takeaways." This approach often leads to rushing through the application due to lack of time and presumes that the congregation will be in top form after a lengthy message. What can students be taught to help avoid this? They can be taught to use a God-centered, application-oriented outline.

The application-oriented outline should stem from the main point of the passage with "special focus on the application of those truths to the current needs of the Church."[78] Others say these are "application-consistent outlines."[79] Such outlines are different from outlines that simply describe or state what someone said or did in the past. The application outline calls for the listener to believe and/or obey the oracles of God and is stressed throughout the message and in the modern-day setting.

What should be included in this type of outline? Assuming that the outline is faithful to the author's intention and it reflects the main point of the passage, it should be stated in the second person imperative (e.g., "you must"). Rarely does one find first person plural teaching in the Bible because the prophets and heralds spoke for God and in God's place. From Jeremiah to John the Baptist, all Bible teachers were simply vehicles for God's Word. In today's culture of "we" preaching and pastoral identification with the woes and struggles of the congregation, this seems odd, but it is biblical and very helpful as each outline point calls the listener to action. The outline is especially beneficial and memorable if the outline points are reiterated before making the transition to the next point of the outline.

Second, the outline points should be directly applicational. How can application-oriented outlines be instituted? Kaiser helps by saying, "First, avoid all use of proper names in the outline except for any of God's names ... Second, never use the past tense of any verb in your sermon outline ... Third, we must not use third-person pronouns ... On the positive side, we should use God's name in the sermon outline."[80] If the outline contains only descriptions about David and Goliath, then the outline is hardly applicable for the modern listener. The teacher should use present tense verbs in full-sentence form that call the listener to think or behave more in line with the Word. Speaking about God in the application outline supports the idea that God is involved and that only His grace enables. Each point then "preaches" by itself and is complete with an appropriate application. The more concrete (versus abstract) and more exhortatory (versus informative) the outline is, the better it will be able to help members of the congregation see how the passage bears on their lives.

Jay Adams describes the last benefit to this approach: it "helps the preacher to accomplish his purpose ... by forcing him—if he follows it—to apply the truth of his passage to the congregation throughout."[81]

3.6 DISCIPLES MUST BE INSTRUCTED THAT THEIR
LESSONS MUST BE CHRIST-CENTERED

The growing tendency in the United States has been to slip into the error of moralistic, "how to" sermons: preachers essentially deliver sermons that call Christians to be more like Christ without showing them Christ and His resources of grace. Instead, Christians need to be reminded that they are "in Christ," and then they should be called to become more who they are. Because God has exalted Christ, all Bible teaching should as well (Philippians 2:9–11).

God is to be lifted up as His Word is preached. Expository students must be taught to preach Jesus Christ, and Him crucified, on a weekly basis without altering the author's intention. Although the subject is complicated, even a cursory exhortation in this area is needed for laymen so that they do not end up teaching the Old Testament and having modern rabbis agree with them.

3.7 DISCIPLES SHOULD BE TAUGHT THE IMPORTANCE OF EXPOSITORY TEACHING

Chapter 8 is devoted entirely to expository preaching, so my comments here will be minimal. The disciples need to understand that "expository preaching is Bible-centered preaching."[82] For laymen, expository preaching could be understood as the proclamation of God's Word in a verse-by-verse or passage-by-passage manner.

Conclusion

Jesus' discipleship included teaching others to verbally pass on Christian truths to others. Since biblical fidelity must be the goal of all teachers, church leaders today do a disservice to their flock if they do not teach basic hermeneutics, exegesis, and homiletics to their men, men who are called to teach their families, evangelize the lost, and in many cases, teach the youth, Sunday school, or even fill the pulpit. The dearth of teachers that many churches experience could be cured by faithful leaders discipling laymen to minister the Word.

Application for laypeople and congregations

1. ASK YOUR PASTOR OR CHURCH LEADER TO HELP YOU BETTER UNDERSTAND THE BIBLE

There may be different levels of discipleship at your church. Ask your pastor for the appropriate place to start.

2. FIND SOMEONE WHO KNOWS LESS THAN YOU DO (ABOUT THE BIBLE) AND TEACH HIM OR HER WHAT YOU HAVE LEARNED

Discipleship receives from the more mature and then gives to those less mature and knowledgeable than you. Start teaching those in your family, and then branch out to the church. Ask a leader to prepare you to disciple other people. Tell him, "When you think I am ready for this weighty responsibility, send a person my way so that I might pour my life into him or her."

3. UNDERSTAND THAT THE DISCIPLE CAN FAIL

While home groups and Bible studies have their place in a local church, what they cannot provide is true accountability. Discipleship that is properly implemented can result in either failure or success. Pass or fail are the two options for each discipleship class. Sheer attendance or auditing will not push the disciple beyond his or her comfort level. There need to be markers to show growth or areas of improvement. Discipleship is often uncomfortable, but it will cause great growth and force you to pray to the God you are studying.

Notes

1 *BDAG*, s.v. "μαθητεύω."

2 All of these words are participles modifying the main verb, "make disciples." In other words, making disciples is done by going, baptizing, and teaching. Unfortunately, the majority of English Bibles translate the participle "going" as a command, "go."

3 **Robert H. Mounce,** *Matthew,* New International Biblical Commentary (Peabody, MA: Hendrickson, 1985, 1991), 268.

4 **D.A. Carson** on Matthew 28:18–20, *Matthew*, vol. 8 of *The Expositor's Bible Commentary*, ed. **Frank E. Gaebelein** and **J.D. Douglas** [CD-ROM] (Grand Rapids: Zondervan, 1984).

5 **Alfred Plummer,** *An Exegetical Commentary on the Gospel According to St Matthew* (London: Robert Scott Roxburghe House, 1928), 435.

6 When Jesus commanded the disciples to preach "repentance for forgiveness of sins" in Luke 24:47, he was not limiting the proclamation to salvation and justification. This message of repentance was the preeminent part of God's message, and that is why Luke focuses upon it.

7 Interestingly, Christ put the center of attention upon His commands and not upon the Old Testament or the Mosaic Law. The disciples were to concentrate on Jesus' words. This focus is buttressed by an earlier saying of His in Matthew 24:35, when Jesus said, "Heaven and earth will pass away, but My words will not pass away."

8 **P.T. O'Brien,** "The Great Commission of Matthew 28:18–20," in *Evangelical Review of Theology* 2 (1978): 254–267.

9 This would surely remind the hearers of the Old Testament, where Yahweh often said, "all that I have commanded you" (Exodus 29:35), "all that the LORD had commanded him" (Deuteronomy 1:3), and "all that I command you" (Deuteronomy 12:11).

10 *Friberg Lexicon,* s.v. "ἔχω."

11 *BDAG,* s.v. "παρατίθημι." See also 1 Timothy 1:18, "This command I entrust to you, Timothy, my son, in accordance with the prophecies previously made concerning you, that by them you fight the good fight."

12 **Gordon D. Fee,** *1 and 2 Timothy, Titus,* New International Biblical Commentary (Peabody, MA: Hendrickson, 1984, 1988), 240.

13 **A.T. Hanson,** *The Pastoral Epistles,* The New Century Bible Commentary (London: Marshal Margon & Scott, 1982), 128.

14 **George W. Knight III,** *Commentary on the Pastoral Epistles,* New International Greek Testament Commentary (Grand Rapids: Eerdmans, 1992), 392.

15 The first level of discipleship would be Paul to Timothy, the second Timothy to faithful men, and the third the faithful men to the next generation.

16 **William Hendricksen,** *I and II Timothy and Titus* (Grand Rapids: Baker, 1957), 246.

17 **Knight,** *Commentary on the Pastoral Epistles,* 391.

18 "The *pastors* and *teachers* are linked here by a single definite article in the Greek, which suggests a close association of functions … the terms describe overlapping functions," **Peter T. O'Brien,** *The Letter to the Ephesians,* The Pillar New Testament Commentary (Grand Rapids: Eerdmans, 1999), 300.

19 *Friberg Lexicon,* s.v. "καταρτισμός."

20 Second Timothy 3:17 uses this word to say that the Word of God makes the "man of God" completely adequate and able for "every good deed."

21 The word translated "equip" is actually used of "setting of a bone" in ancient Greek medical books. See *BDAG*, s.v. "καταρτισμός."

22 O'Brien, *The Letter to the Ephesians*, 301.

23 Lincoln says, "The primary context here in v. 12 is the function and role of Christ" (**Andrew T. Lincoln,** *Ephesians,* Word Biblical Commentary, vol. 42, Dallas: Word Books, 1990, 253).

24 Harold W. Hoehner, *Ephesians: An Exegetical Commentary* (Grand Rapids: Baker, 2002), 550.

25 A. Boyd Luter, Jr., "Discipleship and the Church," in *Bibliotheca Sacra* 137 (July 1980), 274.

26 Michael Lee Abendroth, "Training Laymen to Teach the Bible Expositionally" (Doctoral dissertation: Southern Baptist Theological Seminary, May 2006).

27 Walter C. Kaiser, Jr., *Toward an Exegetical Theology: Biblical Exegesis for Preaching and Teaching* (Grand Rapids: Baker, 1981), 19.

28 Jerry Vines and **David Allen,** "Hermeneutics, Exegesis, and Proclamation," in *Criswell Theological Review* 1/2 (1987), 309.

29 Milton S. Terry, *Biblical Hermeneutics: A Treatise on the Interpretation of the Old and New Testaments* (1885; reprint, Grand Rapids: Zondervan, 1947), 20.

30 Vines and **Allen,** "Hermeneutics, Exegesis, and Proclamation," 310.

31 Kaiser, *Toward an Exegetical Theology*, 47.

32 John Stott, *Between Two Worlds: The Art of Preaching in the Twentieth Century* (Grand Rapids: Eerdmans, 1982), 126.

33 Walter C. Kaiser, Jr., *Preaching and Teaching from the Old Testament* (Grand Rapids: Baker, 2003), 191.

34 Sandra M. Schneiders, "The Paschal Imagination: Objectivity and Subjectivity in New Testament Interpretation," in *Theological Studies* (March 1982), 59.

35 Kaiser, *Toward an Exegetical Theology*, 47.

36 Norman Geisler, "The Relation of Purpose and Meaning in Interpreting Scripture", in *Rightly Divided: Readings in Biblical Hermeneutics*, ed. **Roy B. Zuck** (Grand Rapids: Kregel, 1996), 1.

37 Bernard Ramm, *Protestant Biblical Interpretation: A Textbook on Hermeneutics* (Grand Rapids: Zondervan, 1970), 113.

38 Walter C. Kaiser, Jr., "Legitimate Hermeneutics," in *Inerrancy* (Grand Rapids: Zondervan, 1979), 122.

39 Paul Lee Tan, *The Interpretation of Prophecy* (Winona Lake, IN: Assurance Publishers, 1974), 29.

40 Kaiser, *Toward an Exegetical Theology*, 87.

41 Charles C. Ryrie, *Dispensationalism* (Chicago: Moody Press, 1966), 81.

42 Kaiser, *Preaching and Teaching from the Old Testament*, 52.

43 D.A. Carson, "Must I Learn How to Interpret the Bible?" in *Modern Reformation Magazine* 5/3 ("Scripture," May/June, 1996, updated 2003), 18.

44 Robert L. Thomas, *Evangelical Hermeneutics* (Grand Rapids: Kregel, 2002), 29.

45 Ibid. 173.

46 Vines and **Allen,** "Hermeneutics, Exegesis, and Proclamation," 319.

47 William Barrick, "Expository Preaching–Exegetical Preparation: Dealing with Your Heart and Digging into the Text" (classroom lecture, *The Shepherd's Conference*, March 2003, photocopy), 1.

48 James Barr, *The Semantics of Biblical Language* (New York: Oxford, 1961), 218. An "illegitimate totality transfer" takes place when the full range of a word's meaning is transplanted into another context, oblivious to the new context.

49 Thomas, *Evangelical Hermeneutics*, 64.

50 Kaiser, *Toward an Exegetical Theology*, 135.

51 Roy B. Zuck, *Basic Bible Interpretation* (Colorado Springs: Chariot Victor, 1991), 24.

52 Arturo G. Azurdia III, *Spirit Empowered Preaching* (Fearn, Scotland: Christian Focus, 2003), 29.

53 Charles Bridges, *The Christian Ministry with an Inquiry into the Causes of its Inefficiency* (reprint, Carlisle, PA: Banner of Truth, 1991), 148.

54 Sidney Greidanus, *The Modern Preacher and the Ancient Text: Interpreting and Preaching Biblical Literature* (Grand Rapids: Eerdmans, 1988), 15.

55 Sinclair Ferguson, "Exegesis," in *The Preacher and Preaching: Reviving the Art in the Twentieth Century*, ed. Samuel T. Logan, Jr. (Phillipsburg, NJ: Presbyterian & Reformed, 1986), 193.

56 Ramesh Richard, *Preparing Expository Sermons* (Grand Rapids: Baker, 2001), 18.

57 Miller Maclure, *The Paul's Cross Sermons, 1534–1642* (Toronto: University of Toronto Press, 1958), 165.

58 A. Berkeley Mickelsen, *Interpreting the Bible* (Grand Rapids: Eerdmans, 1963), 5.

59 Haddon W. Robinson, *Making a Difference in Preaching* (Grand Rapids: Baker, 1999), 64–65.

60 Raymond E. Brown, "The *Sensus Plenior* of Sacred Scripture" (S.T.D. diss., St Mary's University, 1955), 92.

61 Ryrie, *Dispensationalism*, 81.

62 Kaiser, *Preaching and Teaching from the Old Testament*, 49.

63 J.H. Jowett, *The Preacher, His Life and Work* (London: Hodder and Stoughton, 1912), 133.

64 Charles Simeon, quoted in **John A. Broadus,** *On the Preparation and Delivery of a Sermon*, 4th ed., rev. Vernon L. Stanfield (San Francisco: Harper and Row, 1979), 38.

65 Haddon W. Robinson, *Biblical Preaching*, 2nd ed. (Grand Rapids: Baker Academic, 1980, 2001), 35.

66 John F. MacArthur, Jr., accessed June 2007 from calvarysbd.com/quotes_pastor.htm.

67 Kaiser, *Toward An Exegetical Theology,* 48.

68 Kaiser, *Preaching and Teaching from the Old Testament*, 177.

69 Henry A. Virkler, "A Proposal for the Transcultural Problem," in *Rightly Divided*, ed. **Roy B. Zuck** (Grand Rapids: Kregel, 1996), 240.

70 Haddon W. Robinson, "The Heresy of Application," in *Leadership Magazine* (Fall 1997), 22.

71 Bryan Chapell, *Christ-Centered Preaching* (Grand Rapids: Baker, 1994), 209.

72 Robinson, "The Heresy of Application," 21.

73 James Stewart, *Heralds of God* (Grand Rapids: Baker, reprinted 1971), 110.

74 Terry, *Biblical Hermeneutics*, 493.

75 Hershael W. York and **Scott A. Blue,** "Is Application Necessary in the Expository Sermon?" in *Southern Baptist Journal of Theology* 3/2 (Summer 1999), 73–74.

76 Richard, *Preparing Expository Sermons*, 48.

77 William D. Thompson, *Preaching Biblically Exegesis and Interpretation* (Nashville: Abingdon Press, 1981), 10.

78 Kaiser, *Toward an Exegetical Theology*, 152.

79 Chapell, *Christ-Centered Preaching*, 146.

80 Kaiser, *Preaching and Teaching from the Old Testament*, 57.

81 Jay Adams, *Preaching with Purpose* (Grand Rapids: Zondervan, 1982), 53.

82 Merrill F. Unger, *Principles of Expository Preaching* (Grand Rapids: Zondervan, 1955), 33.

Jesus preached for a verdict

Are you absolutely confident that you want to preach as Jesus did? Remember that Jesus' preaching provoked others to try to stone Him, muzzle Him, dismiss Him, and accuse Him of blasphemy. Eventually they killed Him for what He preached. Pastors who want to emulate Jesus and preach for a verdict will get negative reactions. Francis Handy cleverly tells pastors of the perils of preaching as Jesus did with these words: "'Safety first' is an excellent motto for the preacher only as he drives his car. His ever-present temptation is to be adroit, to engage in a conspiracy of silence, to avoid issues that are controversial, disturbing, and provocative of trouble—in short, to compromise with his conscience."[1] This chapter seeks to encourage preachers (and laymen) to throw "safety first" overboard and to submit themselves and their pulpit to the Lord in order to preach as Jesus did—for a verdict.

Going for the jugular? What comes naturally and by instinct to lions and dogs is often elusive for some pastors and Bible teachers. When God's Word is unleashed from the pulpit, the results can be devastating. The full-frontal array of God's written artillery explodes on the beachhead of the heart, soul, will, and mind of the congregation with laser-guided accuracy. True biblical preaching goes straight to the heart of the matter. Bible preaching does not "let sleeping dogs lie." Preaching like that of Jesus will never manifest itself in fuzzy, nebulous, hazy, or vague generalities. God's Word proclaimed has more of the effect of a panzer tank than of a warm, cuddly, stuffed toy. Tanks essentially exist to cause change. God, in His love and grace, desires people to change their minds about they way they think about God and themselves. This change is called "repentance." Christ-like preaching ensures that no response from the hearer is a negative response. Actually, the pastor should be happier with an angry response to his message than one of yawning indifference.

The watchwords for a "new" style of preaching today are "relational, inductive, dialogical, narrative, participatory, and interactive." These words typify the latest (albeit reworked—there is nothing new under the sun) philosophy of preaching. I am gravely concerned about the inductive (and all the hybrids stated above) sermon and how it is replacing deductive methodology in evangelical churches. Whether the motives are good (reaching postmoderns or any other people group in any time, place, or culture) or bad (self-promotion or tickling the congregation's ears), the focal point in inductive preaching is not God Himself because the text is secondary. Rather, inductive sermons produce a man-centered philosophy that has the wrong focus (the congregation) on center stage. There is credibility in preaching a message in a style that appropriately matches the original author's genre (it is inappropriate to preach a parable in the same style as one would preach Romans), but this does not mean the deductive sermon should be abandoned.

Preachers in the Bible would shudder at a homiletical approach that advocates "overhearing the gospel" and preaching that somehow manipulates the congregation into choosing the decision you want them to make while never letting it be known that you are the one making the conclusion for them by your methodology. Biblical heralds should sprint from the ethereal, amorphous homiletical style promoted by Walter Brueggemann when he says, "The task and possibility of preaching is to open out the good news of the gospel with alternative modes of speech—speech that is dramatic, artistic, capable of inviting persons to join in another conversation, free of the reason of technique, unencumbered by ontologies that grow abstract, unembarrassed about concreteness."[2]

The twin sister to the inductive message is the story or narrative form of preaching. Eugene L. Lowry would want every sermon to follow this format: "Most books on preaching operate on the common assumption that sermonic organization evolves out of the logic of content ... [I] propose that we begin by regarding the sermon as a homiletical plot, a narrative art form, a sacred story."[3] He even goes so far as to say, "Why not conceive *every* sermon as *narrative*—whether or not a parable or other story is involved?"[4] To that I reply, using his own words, albeit taken out of context, "oops" and "ugh."[5] It is hard for me to fathom such arrogance or ignorance. One brief reading of the epistle of James (many believe this was actually a sermon) will show the reader how far off base Lowry is.

If the desire of the pastor is to be faithful to preach as God's steward, or to preach as Jesus did, he will find that the methodology is plainly revealed in the Bible. Craig Loscalzo sets the reader up to answer improperly when he asks, "How can we preach when traditional approaches don't work?"[6] That is the wrong question. It does not need to be asked, let alone answered. I wonder how Jeremiah would have responded in his ministry? Do we change the medium to attract hearers? Apparently some think so, for they say, "Likewise, we must consider the postmodern idiom if our preaching is to gain a hearing."[7] If this is true, then why are the Pastoral Epistles so quiet about audience retention and accumulation? Will we, as preachers, have to change our philosophy again after postmodernism has run its course and society thinks and acts differently? I stand directly against the notions that say, "I suggest that the argumentative approach, often used in nineteenth-century pulpits, will seldom yield effective results today ... Postmodernism responds better to subjectivity than to objectivity."[8] I have set my face toward the objective (versus subjective), rational (versus post-rational), and authoritative proclamation that leaves drawing the hearers to our Lord. Creating authenticity can be left to the liberals. I prefer to preach as Jesus the Master did.

How did Jesus preach?

Jesus preached for a decision, an ultimatum. His preaching left no room for bystanders to critique His style or method of preaching. His audiences were too busy trying to keep their heads above water as the high-powered words of the Savior flooded them with confrontation. When Jesus preached, there was no "DMZ" (demilitarized zone) where people could hide. When Jesus declared the will of God, people, young and old, Jewish and Samaritan, did not leave as dispassionate, disinterested observers who simply audited His messages. Instead, proverbial fence-sitters were either compelled by the Holy Spirit to repent and obey or they quickly, and of their own doing, sped away to return to their own self-deluded comfort zones.

A sampling of John's Gospel exhibits Christ's preaching style that pushes for a response:

You search the Scriptures because you think that in them you have eternal life; it is these that testify about Me; and you are unwilling to come to Me so that you may have life. I do not receive glory from men; but I know you, that you do not have the love of God in yourselves. I have come in My Father's name, and you do not receive Me; if another comes in his own name, you will receive him. How can you believe, when you receive glory from one another and you do not seek the glory that is from the one and only God? Do not think that I will accuse you before the Father; the one who accuses you is Moses, in whom you have set your hope. For if you believed Moses, you would believe Me, for he wrote about Me. But if you do not believe his writings, how will you believe My words? (John 5:39–47).

Jesus heard that they had put him out, and finding him, He said, "Do you believe in the Son of Man?" (John 9:35).

Jesus said to her [Martha], "I am the resurrection and the life; he who believes in Me will live even if he dies, and everyone who lives and believes in Me will never die. Do you believe this?" (John 11:25–26).

Jesus questioned His listeners with language best described as antithetical black-and-white propositions. The color gray was not in Christ's preaching vocabulary. The jury's verdict needed to be rendered from the will of the person Jesus was addressing. Both the rich young ruler and the Samaritan woman at the well were assaulted with the "all-or-nothing" Jesus.

Preaching for a verdict starts by addressing the mind and pushing it toward a response. The emotions will naturally follow the intellect. Emotional stories may move the feelings, but was that the style of preaching that Jesus employed? Albert Bond notes,

Jesus adopted the normal method of ingress to man's life. The intellect constitutes the first point of contact, without which the other powers of the soul have no control. The emotions can be stirred and the will can be moved only through some intellectual stimulus ... Jesus opened the soul's first gate ... Jesus did not attempt to secure a reasonless response to his teaching.[9]

Jesus preached for a cognitive and rational comprehension that would turn itself into changed attitudes or actions. Many today "preach" for an emotional response without first addressing the mind. Preaching for a judgment must contain preaching to the mind.

Matthew 7:13–14 is a perfect illustration of Christ's preaching style:

Enter through the narrow gate; for the gate is wide and the way is broad that leads to destruction, and there are many who enter through it. For the gate is small and the way is narrow that leads to life, and there are few who find it.

As Jesus concludes the Sermon on the Mount, He confronts His listeners with four warnings, each of which contains contrasts (two ways, 7:13–14; two trees, vv. 15–20; two professions, vv. 21–23; and two foundations, vv. 24–27). Such contrasts are common in Jewish literature and are indicative of Jesus' preaching style that obliges the listener to choose one or the other.

In 7:13–14, Jesus explains the narrow gate, which is restrictive and compressed. It is contrasted with a broad gate, having apt room for accommodation and selling itself as the right entrance to the kingdom of heaven. It is easy to get through this gate. No repentance or faith is necessary; merely a "carry-on-as-is" mindset is needed.

Interestingly, in the Greek, verses 13 and 14 use different words for "narrow." The first "narrow" could also be translated "pent up" or "difficult." The path to heaven is wrought with seemingly insurmountable odds. The second "narrow" actually has the connotation of tribulation caused by persecution. Christ's narrow way is not just compressed and small, but it is made more difficult by opposition. The narrow road leads to eternal life, whereas the broad road leads to eternal destruction. Jesus is throwing the gauntlet down to His hearers. This message demands a response. Just as a line in the sand is meant to force an issue, so Jesus confronts His hearers with the choice between His gracious salvation (narrow gate) or self-righteous religion (broad gate). Tragically, only a few find divine life. Jesus leaves no room for indecision or indifference: eternity hangs in the balance. Elsewhere, Jesus approaches the people in the same direct fashion with these bone-chilling words:

And He was passing through from one city and village to another, teaching, and proceeding on His way to Jerusalem. And someone said to Him, "Lord, are there just a few who are being saved?" And He said to them, "Strive to enter through the narrow door; for many, I tell you, will seek to enter and will not be able. Once the head of the house gets up and shuts the door, and you begin to stand outside and knock on the door, saying, 'Lord, open up to us!' then He will answer and say to you, 'I do not know where you are from.' Then you will begin to say, 'We ate and drank in Your presence, and You taught in our streets'; and He will say, 'I tell you, I do not know where you are from; depart from Me, all you evildoers.' In that place there will be weeping and gnashing of teeth when you see Abraham and Isaac and Jacob and all the prophets in the kingdom of God, but yourselves being thrown out. And they will come from east and west and from north and south, and will recline at the table in the kingdom of God. And behold, some are last who will be first and some are first who will be last" (Luke 13:22–30).

The premise that Jesus preached for a verdict can be attested by letting Jesus' words resonate for themselves. Read the following parable by Jesus and ask, "Was this preaching for a verdict?" Detailed polemics to decide the answer are needless.

"But what do you think? A man had two sons, and he came to the first and said, 'Son, go work today in the vineyard.' And he answered, 'I will not'; but afterward he regretted it and went. The man came to the second and said the same thing; and he answered, 'I will, sir'; but he did not go. Which of the two did the will of his father?" They said, "The first." Jesus said to them, "Truly I say to you that the tax collectors and prostitutes will get into the kingdom of God before you. For John came to you in the way of righteousness and you did not believe him; but the tax collectors and prostitutes did believe him; and you, seeing this, did not even feel remorse afterward so as to believe him" (Matthew 21:28–32).

George Buttrick tries to put out the fire of Christ's preaching style with bold over-generalizing: "Jesus taught in parables because a parable disarms, and wins, when an argument might alienate."[10] Yet the parable quoted above hardly fits the mold of Buttrick's liberal Jesus. Even the parables of the Son of Man were verdict-driven.

The most impressive display from Jesus was His direct, confrontational question to the disciples. The story is familiar:

Now when Jesus came into the district of Caesarea Philippi, He was asking His disciples, "Who do people say that the Son of Man is?" And they said, "Some say John the Baptist; and others, Elijah; but still others, Jeremiah, or one of the prophets." He said to them, "But who do you say that I am?" Simon Peter answered, "You are the Christ, the Son of the living God." And Jesus said to him, "Blessed are you, Simon Barjona, because flesh and blood did not reveal this to you, but My Father who is in heaven" (Matthew 16:13–17).

The preaching was so difficult that the answer had to be given by the omniscient first person of the Trinity! Jesus deliberately proclaimed the truth of God so that obedience would come only by divine intervention and assistance. Do you teach the Bible in this manner?

Application for preachers, elders, leaders, and Bible teachers

1. ALWAYS INCLUDE A "SO WHAT?" IN EACH SERMON

I often write the words "So what?" at the end of my sermons so that I will remember to press the truth of God to the consciences of the people. The difference between preaching and teaching is this: teaching informs the mind, while preaching both informs the mind and challenges the will. Teaching says, "Here is some information," and preaching says, "You must believe this information with all your heart!"

Jim Elliff's advice is worth repeating:

As you preach, some will caution you to be balanced. It is a wise thought if understood correctly. But there is another way to look at the idea of balance. Why not try to balance the years of weak, half-hearted platitudinal sermonettes your people have been hearing with good sound doctrine? Every sermon cannot be balanced. You should not expect it to be. Jesus' sermons were not. Please do not fear leaving the people with some question. I would think that it would be a very good thing for people to leave the building on Sundays with a head full of questions. At least they are thinking again and not just nodding. At least it is stirring them up from their sleep. You couldn't be more like Jesus in your preaching if you leave them wondering and working through the questions. Jesus left head-scratching wherever he went. Do not fear being like Jesus.[11]

In other words, preach for a verdict, as Christ did! If the congregation thought and acted perfectly, there would be no reason to correct or confront them with preaching. Challenging truth is the most loving gift you could ever give your congregation.

The "So what?" can be strategically placed throughout the sermon, but it will often find its culmination at the end of your message. The implication is that time and thought must be invested in the closing of your proclamation in order to highlight the "So what?" question (and answer). Sermonic conclusions made up on the fly or thrown-together recaps of the outline rarely bring the congregation to a moment of decision.[12] Time and effort expended in the crafting of the end of the sermon will pay large dividends when preaching for a verdict. Even Bryan Chapell, a full-blown Calvinist who trusts in the sovereignty of God, recognizes the need for a preacher's due diligence in the preparation of a sermon. He says with insight, "We cannot too strongly emphasize the need for preparation since too many preachers delay constructing a conclusion until they are worn out from preparing the meat of the sermon. As a result, these preachers are tempted to extemporize (rationalized as letting the Holy Spirit inspire) that portion of the sermon that holds the potential for greatest impact."[13] While one might disagree with the term "inspire," his point is well taken. David Larsen adds, "I recommend to my students that they spend two-thirds of their time on the last one-third of their message."[14] Sermons that finish well need time in the oven of preparation so that they will be cooked to perfection. Strangely, even the liberal Buttrick comprehends the necessity of thinking through your sermon's ending, saying, "Conclusions are governed by intention."[15] Out of all the possible ways to end a sermon (direct personal appeal, practical application, summary or recapitulation, appeal to imagination, the use of a short poem or hymn stanza, a final illustration, an apt quotation, return to the introduction, personal testimony, or some concluding suspension[16]), the preacher would imitate Jesus if he would regularly preach for a verdict.

2. TEACH YOUR CONGREGATION THIS PARADIGM:
REVELATION (OF GOD) DEMANDS A RESPONSE

The church will readily grasp this truth. When God speaks, He does not speak so that He can hear Himself speak; He speaks to His people to educate, rebuke, or proclaim His truth to them. The proper attitude to the Lord's voice is quick obedience. As the slogan goes, "God's Word is not just for our information, it is also for our transformation." When the God of the universe speaks, He expects to be heard and obeyed.

3. USE THE SECOND PERSON IMPERATIVE ("YOU") WHEN YOU PREACH

One set of scholars counted the times Jesus used the second person imperative during His Sermon on the Mount: "Let's reconsider the Sermon on the Mount. We've already mentioned Jesus' use of direct discourse (221 times 'you' or 'your') and questions (nineteen) in this eighteen-minute sermon …"[17] Why are preachers today so apt to say "we" and not "you"? "We" preaching is conveyed as sharing instead of declaring.

J.C. Ryle ponders:

Remember good Bishop Villiers saying that "we" was a word kings and corporations should use, and they alone, but that parish clergymen should always talk of "I" and "you" … I declare I never can understand what the famous pulpit "we" means. Does the preacher who all through his sermon keeps saying "we" mean himself and the bishop? or himself and the Church? or himself and the congregation? or himself and the Early Fathers? or himself and the Reformers? or himself and all the wise men in the world? or, after all, does he only mean myself, plain "John Smith" or "Thomas Jones?" … If you begin to talk in the vague plural number of what "we" ought to do, many of your hearers do not know what you are driving at, and whether you are speaking to yourself or them. I charge and entreat my younger brethren in the ministry not to forget this point. Do try to be as direct as possible. Never mind what people say of you.[18]

Ask yourself this question: "What did the biblical preachers such as John the Baptist, Jeremiah, Peter, or Paul do?" They preached with the second person imperative: "You must." For example:

But Peter, taking his stand with the eleven, raised his voice and declared to them: "Men of Judea and all you who live in Jerusalem, let this be known to you and give heed to my words" (Acts 2:14).

Men of Israel, listen to these words: Jesus the Nazarene, a man attested to you by God with miracles and wonders and signs which God performed through Him in your midst, just as you yourselves know—this Man, delivered over by the predetermined plan and foreknowledge of God, you nailed to a cross by the hands of godless men and put Him to death. But God raised Him up again, putting an end to the agony of death, since it was impossible for Him to be held in its power (Acts 2:22–24).

Brethren, I may confidently say to you regarding the patriarch David that he both died and was buried, and his tomb is with us to this day (Acts 2:29).

"Therefore let all the house of Israel know for certain that God has made Him both Lord and Christ—this Jesus whom you crucified." Now when they heard this, they were pierced to the heart, and said to Peter and the rest of the apostles, "Brethren, what shall we do?" (Acts 2:36–37).

Elijah came near to all the people and said, "How long will you hesitate between two opinions? If the LORD is God, follow Him; but if Baal, follow him." But the people did not answer him a word (1 Kings 18:21).

Teach your flock that God preaches to you all week in your study, and now, as God's herald, you preach to them.

4. CONSTRUCT YOUR HOMILETICAL OUTLINE POINTS WITH APPLICATION

The best method for homiletical application is to incorporate it directly into the outline of the sermon. That guarantees that the application will be intricately involved throughout the entire message. It will not be rushed through at the end or treated like an "add-on" or appendage. John A. Broadus said, "The application of the sermon is not merely an appendage to the discussion or a subordinate part of it, but is the main thing to be done."[19] Application-oriented outlines drive home each "point" to the hearers as part of the sermon. Hershael W. York and Bert Decker concur: "We still believe that the real 'point' of the sermon is *always* application, so let's just be honest and reflect that in the points of the sermon ... Another common mistake is to save all the application of the sermon for the end."[20] Because "exposition assumes the duty of exhorting the people of God to apply the truths revealed in Scripture not because of the opinion of experts but because of the instruction of God's Word,"[21] I want to implore people to obey or think differently right from the starting gun of the sermon, all the way through it, and at the end.

Outline points should seek to be God-centered, in the present tense, in complete or full sentences, and distinctly practical.[22] This is similar to what Chapell calls the "Application Consistent Outline."[23] Chapell gives further advice, stating, "Experienced preachers also usually take passives and the nots out of main points. Application clauses worded with passive verbs do not exhort people to do anything, they simply state what happens to people—usually in the uninvolving third person ... Make sure people know what the Bible intends as well as what it prohibits."[24] Avoid "the trap of making merely descriptive outlines—main points should be hortatory in nature."[25]

Outlines that reflect God's intention will force the preacher to more accurately tie his application to the message. Haddon Robinson says that there is heresy preached in evangelical pulpits because pastors wrongly apply the verse. Robinson calls this "The Heresy of Application."[26] Practical exhortation must find its source in the text itself; otherwise, the propensity to drift away from the authorial intent grows more likely. Instead, interject your application all the way through the sermon while making sure it is God's intended application. C.H. Spurgeon said,

I used to put the application at the end of my sermon. That is a good rule; but as I found sinners rather sleepy at the close, I generally now, after a piece of doctrine for the building up of the saints, let fly at sinners when they are not expecting it. The shot takes them unawares ... Our doctrines are not the dry bones of crusty old theologues, but the living and life-changing words of God! It should be natural to mix our doctrine with appeals both to the lost and the saved. If it burns in us, it will be most certainly so.[27]

Danny Akin has compiled the following series of outlines. Notice the progression toward application.

Six hypothetical outlines (first five by Walter Liefield and sixth by Danny Akin)[28]

Type one: Description
1. The Lord, our Light
2. The Lord, our Salvation
3. The Lord, our Refuge

Type two: Declaration
1. The Lord is our Light
2. The Lord is our Salvation
3. The Lord is our Refuge

Type three: Explanation
1. What does it mean that the Lord is our Light?
2. What does it mean that the Lord is our Salvation?
3. What does it mean that the Lord is our Refuge?

Type four: Exhortation
1. Let the Lord be your Light
2. Let the Lord be your Salvation
3. Let the Lord be your Refuge

Type five: Application
1. How the Lord can be our daily Light in darkness
2. How the Lord can be our Savior when we sense our guilt
3. How the Lord can be our strong Refuge when we feel besieged

Type six: Exhortation with Application
1. Let the Lord be your daily Light in darkness
2. Let the Lord be your Savior when you sense your guilt
3. Let the Lord be your strong Refuge when you feel besieged

5. STICK TO THE MAIN THEME OF YOUR PASSAGE

When Bible teachers have eighteen teaching points, it is nearly impossible to preach for a verdict. Distill your sermon to stress the main point of the passage and propose a verdict question or scenario for that single key point. Comprise your weekly messages around the main theme, and then continually reinforce the theme throughout each entire message. Every sub-point should reflect its submission to the dominant purpose of the text, so that when people walk out of the Worship Service, if they were asked, "What was the sermon about today?" they would be able to answer it. Preferably, they would respond with a sentence that reflects and communicates the thrust of the passage that was preached.

To aid you in this endeavor of keeping continuity via a central theme, try implementing Chapell's "wraparound."[29] He defines it this way: "A highly professional way of concluding is to hearken back to material mentioned in the sermon's introduction (or other earlier portions of the message)." This simple technique is beneficial to the listener and keeps the Bible teacher focused on the foremost and central theme or themes. This is the same thing that York and Decker call the "*inclusio*, the bracketing effect that comes when we reintroduce an earlier subject."[30] This conscious effort weaves the main point into both the introduction and the conclusion.

Application for laypeople and congregations

1. BE READY TO BE CHALLENGED FROM THE PULPIT ON A WEEKLY BASIS

As you listen to a sermon, make it your main goal to listen to the sermon for the exaltation of the triune God. Remember He has exalted His Word. Desire holiness when you hear preaching. Holiness will always lead to happiness, while happiness rarely yields holiness. Every week your pastor will be looking to the Holy Spirit to grant you a response of obedience to His Word. Learn to expect preaching like this from your heralding pastor. John Stott grasps the nature of the pastor when he writes, "The herald does not just preach good news, whether men will hear or whether they will forbear. No. The proclamation issues in an appeal. The herald expects a response."[31] You should expect to be challenged.

2. REALIZE THAT "FEELING GOOD" IS NOT AN
ADMIRABLE GOAL WHILE LISTENING TO A SERMON

Suppress the idea of yearning to feel good after a sermon. Feeling good may come at a later time after God grants repentance, but it is not a proper barometer to gauge the sermon's value. In 1958, Dr Norman Pittenger wrote "A Critique of C.S. Lewis." He said that C.S. Lewis did not really care for the Sermon on the Mount. Lewis responded with a "Rejoinder to Dr Pittenger." Lewis said, "As to 'caring for' the Sermon on the Mount, if 'caring for' here means 'liking' or enjoying, I suppose no one 'cares for' it. Who can like being knocked flat on his face by a sledge hammer? I can hardly imagine a more deadly spiritual condition than that of a man who can read that passage with tranquil pleasure."[32] Feeling good should be relegated to the time after the conviction and confession of sin. You should "feel good" that God conforms His people to the likeness of Jesus Christ by firm preaching.

3. STUDY THE "HARD SAYINGS" OF JESUS

A quick concordance study of "hard" or "difficult" sayings in the Gospels will award the reader refreshment as he or she is reminded of Christ's confrontational style and His hearers' acknowledgement of this. Regularly read Matthew, Mark, Luke, John, and Revelation 2–3 so that you can sit under the preaching of Jesus.

4. KNOW THAT PREACHING FOR A VERDICT
IS GOOD FOR YOUR SPIRITUAL CONDITION

Thank the Lord for loving you enough not to leave you in your current spiritual condition. God has graciously granted you a faithful Bible teacher to be God's instrument in delivering the Lord's transforming truth. Remember the children's ditty "Sticks and stones may break my bones, but words may never hurt me"? When it comes to preaching, I suggest it should be adjusted to "Sticks and stones may break my bones, but biblical words are sure to convict and sanctify me." Ask the Lord to help you appreciate His love for you as He prunes you through preaching. Douglas Wilson, in one of my all-time favorite quotes, compares congregational members and their attitudes toward preaching that demands a verdict, pronouncing:

We live in an era which places a high value on hardness of heart. We can tell this by our love of soft teaching ... We like to believe that this love of soft words, words which will trouble neither the mind nor heart, nor anything in between, is a deep love of tenderness. Such a conviction flatters us, but our love is actually the opposite of tenderness. If our hearts were a slab of concrete, and we wanted to keep them that way, our desire to have them caressed with a feather duster would exhibit no love of tenderness, but rather the contrary. The one who really wanted a tender heart would be calling for the jackhammer. Hard words, hard teaching, are the jackhammer of God. It takes a great deal to break up our hard hearts, and the God of all mercy is willing to do it. But He always does it according to His Word, and His Word is not as easy on us as we would like. "Is not my word like as a fire? Saith the LORD; and like a hammer that breaketh the rock in pieces?" (Jer. 23:29). When Christians call for smooth words, easy words, the result is hard people. When we submit to hard words, we become the tenderhearted of God. But let soft words have their way in a congregation, let soft words dominate the pulpit, and hardness of heart begins to manifest itself in countless ways—but the common denominator is always that of granite hearts. Marriages dissolve, heresies proliferate, parents abandon children, churches split, children heap contempt on their parents, quarrels erupt on the elder board and in the choir, bitterness, rancor, envy, and malice about—and all because the people will not abide that loathsome jackhammer, "Thou shalt not."[33]

Notes

1 **Francis J. Handy,** *Jesus the Preacher* (New York: Abingdon-Cokesbury Press, 1946), 92.

2 **Walter Brueggemann,** *Finally Comes The Poet* (Minneapolis: Augsburg Fortress, 1989), 3.

3 **Eugene L. Lowry,** *The Homiletical Plot* (Louisville: Westminster John Knox, 2001), xix–xxi.

4 Ibid. 13.

5 Ibid. 26.

6 **Craig A. Loscalzo,** *Apologetic Preaching* (Downers Grove: InterVarsity Press, 2000), back cover.

7 Ibid. 21.

8 Ibid. 39.

9 **Albert Richmond Bond,** *The Master Preacher* (New York: American Tract Society, 1910), 50.

10 **George Buttrick,** "Matthew: Text, Exegesis, and Exposition," in *General Articles on the New Testament; Matthew; Mark,* vol. 7 of ed. **George Buttrick** *et.al., The Interpreter's Bible* (New York: Abingdon Press, 1951), 408.

11 Jim Elliff, "Serious Preaching (and Listening)," accessed from www.ccwonline.org/spreaching.html.

12 When I say "decision," I do not mean anything remotely related to decisional regeneration, altar calls, or any other Finney-like expression of evangelism. Congregational consent to the Word of God preached is the goal.

13 Bryan Chapell, *Christ-Centered Preaching* (Grand Rapids: Baker, 1994), 251.

14 David L. Larsen, *The Anatomy of Preaching: Identifying the Issues in Preaching Today* (Grand Rapids: Kregel, 1989), 121.

15 David G. Buttrick, *Homiletic Moves and Structures* (Philadelphia: Fortress Press, 1987), 97.

16 Larsen, *The Anatomy of Preaching*, 123–128.

17 Ralph L. Lewis with **Gregg Lewis,** *Inductive Preaching* (Westchester, IL: Crossway, 1983), 147.

18 J.C. Ryle, *The Upper Room* (Carlisle, PA: Banner of Truth, 1970), 46–47.

19 John A. Broadus, *On the Preparation and Delivery of Sermons,* ed. J.B. Weatherspoon (New York: Harper and Row, 1944), 210.

20 Hershael W. York and **Bert Decker,** *Preaching with Bold Assurance: A Solid and Enduring Approach to Engaging Exposition* (Nashville: Broadman & Holman, 2003), 142.

21 Chapell, *Christ-Centered Preaching*, 79.

22 Danny Akin, D.Min. class on New Testament preaching, Southern Baptist Theological Seminary, 2004.

23 Chapell, *Christ-Centered Preaching*, 146.

24 Ibid. 147.

25 Ibid. 149.

26 Haddon W. Robinson, "The Heresy of Application," in *Leadership Magazine* (Fall 1997), 21.

27 C.H. Spurgeon, quoted in **Elliff,** "Serious Preaching".

28 Danny Akin, class lecture, "New Testament Preaching," Southern Baptist Theological Seminary, 2004.

29 Chapell, *Christ-Centered Preaching*, 250.

30 York and **Decker,** *Preaching with Bold Assurance*, 158.

31 John Stott, *Between Two Worlds: The Art of Preaching in the Twentieth Century* (Grand Rapids: Eerdmans, 1982), 31.

32 C.S. Lewis, *God in the Dock*, ed. Walter Hooper (Grand Rapids: Eerdmans, 1970), 181–182.

33 Douglas Wilson, *Mother Kirk: Essays and Forays in Practical Ecclesiology* (Moscow, ID: Canon Press, 2001), 77.

Jesus was an expository preacher

What is expository preaching?

There is some debate as to whether Jesus proclaimed God's truth expositionally. One of the contributors to this dispute is in the very definition of the term "expository preaching." Expository preaching is a fluid term with many different definitions. Let's examine a few descriptions of exposition and then discuss whether Jesus practiced this methodology according to these definitions. First, Jerry Vines and Jim Shaddix define expository preaching as "the process of laying open a biblical text in such a way that its original meaning is brought to bear on the lives of contemporary listeners."[1] Second, Ramesh Richard describes expository preaching as "the contemporization of the central proposition of a biblical text that is derived from proper methods of interpretation and declared through effective means of communication to inform minds, instruct hearts, and influence behavior toward godliness."[2] Third, Haddon W. Robinson claims that "At its best, expository preaching is the presentation of biblical truth, derived from and transmitted through a historical, grammatical, Spirit-guided study of a passage in its context, which the Holy Spirit applies first to the life of the preacher and then through him to his congregation."[3]

What expository preaching is not

At one extreme, expository preaching is not the proclamation of a series of cross-references assembled without exegesis. At the other extreme, it is not a grouping of scholarly, exegetical data that has no theme or homiletical rhetoric. Richard Mayhue describes what expository preaching is not, saying, "It is not a chopped-up collection of grammatical findings and quotations from commentaries without a fusing of the same into a smooth, flowing, interesting, and compelling message."[4] Lastly, it is not a rambling discussion about the Bible; rather, as Merrill Unger says, "It is emphatically not preaching about the Bible, but preaching the Bible. 'What saith the Lord' is the alpha and the omega of expository preaching. It begins in the Bible and ends in the Bible and all that intervenes springs from the Bible. In other words, expository preaching is Bible-centered preaching."[5]

Summary

I would simply define expository preaching as a style or method of preaching God's Word which seeks to logically "expose" the biblical text to the mind and will of the congregation. The "man of God" is to passionately open up, uncover, and lay bare the rich truths contained in Holy Writ, and then he must urge the people of God to both understand and obey the truth they have just learned, doing all this to the glory of Jesus Christ. Expository preaching is essentially preaching the biblical text to people with accuracy and interpretational fidelity to the original meaning so that hearers will understand who God is and what He requires. Expository preaching is preaching given by a man who, above all else, wants to glorify His Lord by studying a passage to find out what it means to God (so many wrongly think that the object during study is "me") and then persuasively proclaiming that truth, in context, to a group of His sheep with an earnest desire to see God exalted.

Did Jesus preach this way? This is not really a fair question because, for the most part, Jesus spoke without quoting or referring to Old Testament texts. That is to say, Jesus, as the incarnate Word, spoke directly as God, and for God. Jesus did not need to habitually quote chapter and verse (although He could have done so). Instead, Jesus was God's living exposition and therefore He, as He spoke and preached, always exposed people to the true meaning of the will of God, whether or not He referred to the Old Testament.

To a large degree, based on the above definitions, Jesus was an expository preacher. While He did not preach "through a book of the Old Testament" sequentially, verse by verse over three years, He did always expose people to the God-intended meaning of the text and implore them to obey. Jesus never imposed an extra-biblical meaning on Holy Scriptures. Let's specifically look at Christ's preaching from the Old Testament.

Examples of Jesus' preaching

Two Gospel passages tower over all the others when it comes to elucidating the marvelous power of Jesus Christ's preaching. But do they exhibit expository preaching? Let's study both passages.

LUKE 4

And Jesus returned to Galilee in the power of the Spirit, and news about Him spread through all the surrounding district. And He began teaching in their synagogues and was praised by all. And He came to Nazareth, where He had been brought up; and as was His custom, He entered the synagogue on the Sabbath, and stood up to read. And the book of the prophet Isaiah was handed to Him. And He opened the book and found the place where it was written,

"The Spirit of the LORD is upon Me,
Because He anointed Me to preach the gospel to the poor.
He has sent Me to proclaim release to the captives,
And recovery of sight to the blind,
To set free those who are oppressed,
To proclaim the favorable year of the LORD."

And He closed the book, gave it back to the attendant and sat down; and the eyes of all in the synagogue were fixed on Him. And He began to say to them, "Today this Scripture has been fulfilled in your hearing." And all were speaking well of Him, and wondering at the gracious words which were falling from His lips; and they were saying, "Is this not Joseph's son?" (Luke 4:14–22).

Many historical events have been so significant that I wish I could have been there to experience them in time and space. The account in Luke 4 is one of those events. The word that best describes the scenario is "stunning." As Luke is prone to do, he mentions the particular ministry of the Holy Spirit and how He, after driving Jesus into the wilderness for satanic temptations (Luke 4:1 ff.), now impels Jesus to Galilee for public ministry.

This Spirit-driven day was going to prove exceptional. Jesus arrives for worship and most likely is recognized by the leaders. His fame is preceding

Him. They ask Him to be one of the Scripture readers for the day. A servant opens the box containing the scrolls, chooses the appropriate one, unwraps it, and delivers it to Jesus. Jesus stands in traditional reverence for God's Word. Custom dictated standing while reading God's Word, except when Esther was read during the feast of Purim.[6] Jesus, in the town of His upbringing, is handed the scroll opened at Isaiah. Writing about the scrolls, physician Luke vividly employs the Greek word translated "unrolled" or "opened," a medical word used to describe the "opening up" of a patient's body ready for surgery.[7] Jesus was about to open up more than a scroll; He was going to open up the sluice gates of the Messianic ministry! The LXX uses the same word, "spread it out," when Hezekiah received a letter and read it, then took it and exposed it to the LORD (2 Kings 19:14). Just as a feast is "spread out" on the table, so now Jesus was about to give His listeners a spiritual feast that they would not soon forget.

Whether Jesus chose Isaiah 61:1–2 purposely or whether it was an assigned reading for the day, the effect was apocalyptic. There would be no reason for Jesus to deviate from custom and pick a different selection, so it was likely the next passage to be read in the synagogue. Divine orchestration is seen as Jesus reads a passage in Isaiah about the Messianic hope, which is really about Himself. In Luke 4:18, Jesus says, "He has sent me to proclaim release to the captives ..." He purposefully changes the tense of the verb "has sent" in LXX to a perfect active indicative, signifying that He Himself is the One God has sent. Jesus effectively says, "This Messiah is in your midst—I am He!" Jesus Himself will grant liberty to captives and He will release prisoners. He will heal and help the oppressed. He is the object of Isaiah's prophecy. Now is the time for the prophecy to be fulfilled. The Messianic era starts today. Jesus Himself will glorify the Father by preaching the good news to sinners.

With a dramatic close, Jesus quietly rolls up the scroll, gives it back to the attendant, and sits down. Why did He sit down? The Jews knew that He sat down to teach them. That is why they were all looking at Him. The Jewish rabbis would sit to teach their disciples (Matthew 5:1ff.), so the people had their eyes riveted upon Jesus for His Messianic message. They were intently observing Him because it was now time for the teaching of the Word. Marvin R. Vincent reports that the prophetic readings in the synagogues were followed by a discourse.[8] They were waiting for Him to begin the expositional message based upon Isaiah 61.

They were literally staring at Him. With spellbound, rapt focus they stared at Him. They were mesmerized. Paul used the word here translated "fixed" in 2 Corinthians 3:7 and 13 to describe the people gazing on Moses after he returned from Sinai with a glowing face. Jesus had dropped the atomic bomb, "Today, your Messiah, predicted by Isaiah, has come, and I am your King." Do you think He had their attention?

It seems that Luke recorded only the first sentence of Jesus' "sermon": "Today this Scripture has been fulfilled in your hearing" (Luke 4:21). Luke declared that this sentence was what "He began to say to them," indicating there was more that was said. Albert Barnes supports this interpretation when he records, "It is probable that he said much 'more' than is here recorded, but Luke has preserved only the 'substance' of his discourse. This was the 'amount' or 'sum' of his sermon, or his explanation of the passage, that it was now receiving its accomplishment."[9] It is inconceivable that Jesus' discourse would have been about the Sabbath, tithing, or fasting. With the Messiah sitting in front of them (or at least someone claiming to be the Messiah), the people surely heard further elucidation of the person and future work of Christ. Vincent likewise writes that Jesus "expounded" Isaiah 61:1–2.[10]

How did they respond? Their twofold response consisted of praise and wonder. How could such words of grace come from a local carpenter's son? Without question, the reputation and "fame" of Jesus were on the upswing.

Was this an exposition? Was it expository preaching? The answer is "yes." Jesus exposed the Jews to the proper meaning of the biblical text, and He surely did it so they would believe Him. Robert Mounce explains, "They needed to be taught the implications of the announcement." [11] The real Messiah would additionally express clarifying comments so the people could fully understand the ramifications of the Scripture reading and the local man Jesus. F.B. Meyer believes this was exposition, saying,

We cannot found an argument upon this single act, but it is at least significant that the Lord gave His sanction to the systematic reading and consideration of the inspired Word in His earliest sermon. Our Lord was also careful to consider the text in relation to the context and the whole tenor and teaching of Scripture. The habit of taking a little snippet of a verse from any part of the Bible and making it the subject of discourse, exposes the preacher to the danger of an unbalanced statement of truth, which is very prejudicial. Nothing is more perilous than the partial knowledge of God's truth, which is based on sentences torn from their rock-bed and viewed in isolation from their setting.[12]

Mayhue agrees, calling Christ's actions in Luke 4:16–22 the "expounding of Isa. 61:1–2 in the synagogue ..."[13]

LUKE 24:25–27
The second passage highlighting Jesus' expository preaching is Luke 24:25–27, which records Jesus saying,

And He said to them, "O foolish men and slow of heart to believe in all that the prophets have spoken! Was it not necessary for the Christ to suffer these things and to enter into His glory?" Then beginning with Moses and with all the prophets, He explained to them the things concerning Himself in all the Scriptures.

Jesus is chiding Cleopas and his companions for not seeing both sides of the Messianic prophecies, especially those that included His suffering. He uses the first two parts of the Hebrew Bible ("Moses and ... all the prophets") to exposit and expound these forgotten truths to them.

Does "explained" mean "translated" or "expounded"? Alfred Plummer says, "In Acts ix. 36 and 2 Mac. i. 36 the verb is used of interpreting a foreign language."[14] On the other hand, Thayer says it means, "to unfold the meaning of what is said, explain, expound: τι, Luke 24:27; absolutely, 1 Cor. 12:30; 14:5, 13, 27."[15] Which one is it? Jesus is not translating from one language to another, but rather clarifying and explaining the Scriptures to them.

Joel Green asks a very insightful question: "Which texts does Jesus exegete for his companions? We are not told of the specifics, but the implication Luke leaves us is that it does not matter. The pattern exemplified by Moses and the prophets is consummated in a Messiah who suffers. Likewise, all of the Scriptures have their fulfillment in a Messiah who suffers."[16] Interestingly, the focus is more on the exposition and not on the exact text or substance of what exactly Jesus said. Jesus wants them to fully absorb and comprehend the significance of the Bible, so He gives them an explication. He wants them to know and recognize what the Bible really says. Jesus exposes His hearers to the real meaning of the Old Testament. Norval Geldenhuys adds,

And then the Saviour, who knows the Word of God perfectly, because of His intimate union with the Spirit who is its Primary Author, expounded to them in broad outline all the Scriptures that referred to Him, from the first books of the Old Testament and right through to the end. With burning hearts (verse 32), but still unaware that it was Jesus Himself who was teaching them, they listened to His incomparable exposition of the deepest contents of the Old Testament.[17]

There is little doubt that Jesus practiced an expository explanation of the Old Testament. If it was not exposition, then our current definitions of expository preaching need to be redefined to include the methods of Jesus Himself. While sequential messages in one single book cannot be proven with the words of Jesus, Jesus gives us a clear pattern that preachers must faithfully speak for God from the text in order that people will understand the Scriptures and obey them.

Luke chapters 4 and 24 fit with Richard Mayhue's bare minimums for expositional preaching, that is: Christ's messages were based only on Scripture, contained proper exegesis, properly interpreted the Word in context, explained the authorial intent of the passage, and pushed His hearers to obey. [18]

Would Jesus have had any Old Testament examples to draw upon?

It is advantageous to scrutinize the Old Testament to see if expository preaching was implemented there. After all, the Old Testament was Jesus' "Bible." He would have known it experientially (as a child, student, and rabbi) and intrinsically (as the Son of God who authored the Word). Does the Old Testament teach or model expository preaching?

Expository preaching was not something that made its debut in the New

Testament Gospels. The following two Old Testament passages would have been very familiar to Jesus and would have inspired Him to teach in an expository fashion. These passages describing two of the most memorable preaching events in the Old Testament amplify exposition and remind us of the continuity of expository preaching.

NEHEMIAH 8:8

What a joyous occasion it must have been for Ezra to have the opportunity to proclaim the Word of God! To have the Word of Yahweh back into the hands of the people, particularly after such a long time without any comfort or guidance by revelation, must have been glorious. The text reads:

And all the people gathered as one man at the square which was in front of the Water Gate, and they asked Ezra the scribe to bring the book of the law of Moses which the LORD had given to Israel. Then Ezra the priest brought the law before the assembly of men, women and all who could listen with understanding, on the first day of the seventh month. He read from it before the square which was in front of the Water Gate from early morning until midday, in the presence of men and women, those who could understand; and all the people were attentive to the book of the law. Ezra the scribe stood at a wooden podium which they had made for the purpose. And beside him stood Mattithiah, Shema, Anaiah, Uriah, Hilkiah, and Maaseiah on his right hand; and Pedaiah, Mishael, Malchijah, Hashum, Hashbaddanah, Zechariah and Meshullam on his left hand. Ezra opened the book in the sight of all the people for he was standing above all the people; and when he opened it, all the people stood up. Then Ezra blessed the LORD the great God. And all the people answered, "Amen, Amen!" while lifting up their hands; then they bowed low and worshiped the LORD with their faces to the ground. Also Jeshua, Bani, Sherebiah, Jamin, Akkub, Shabbethai, Hodiah, Maaseiah, Kelita, Azariah, Jozabad, Hanan, Pelaiah, the Levites, explained the law to the people while the people remained in their place. They read from the book, from the law of God, translating to give the sense so that they understood the reading (Nehemiah 8:1–8).

There is some scholarly debate regarding the method of this reading described in verse 8. H.G.M. Williamson thinks that:

By establishing that this verse is a concluding summary, we have already fixed the general parameters for its interpretation, namely the subjects for each verb, and the fact that the actions recorded are the same as those already explained, rather than fresh developments ... Continuous reading would have been exhausting for reader and audience alike. As it was, the text was broken down into sensible units. This gave opportunity for others to share the physical task of reading with Ezra and for him to select those portions of the Law that he deemed most appropriate.[19]

This description helps the reader to understand the methodology—the "how" of such an enterprise—a little more. F. Charles Fensham further elaborates on the undertaking, saying, "These thirteen persons were Levites who were responsible for the interpretation of the law. How it was done is not said. Every one of them might have taken a group of the congregation to explain the law. The Levites played here approximately the same role as ascribed to them in 2 Chr. 17:7–9."[20]

The more important issue is not the process or manner of priests or Levites in breaking the text down (the mechanics of the situation) but rather what the speakers actually said. Did Ezra "translate" or did he "explain"? Was he acting like an expositor or like a decoder who deciphered the text from one language and then spoke it in another? The New American Standard Bible interprets the Hebrew verb פֹרֵשׁ (plural participle, masculine singular) as "translating." This opinion is shared by many scholars, such as D.J. Clines, who summarizes this simple translation view:

The traditional interpretation has been that they [the Levites] translated or paraphrased the Hebrew text into Aramaic, which would have been more easily understood by the ex-Babylonian Jews ... This may well have been the case, though the text says nothing directly about translation, and some have thought that the Levites' task was not translation but explanation (for their teaching function). The key word is *meporas* (v. 8), clearly, which literally signifies "separated, split up," i.e. with distinct pronunciation, or, more probably, with pauses between each verse.[21]

Edwin Yamauchi, agreeing with Clines' translation view, places similar weight on the Aramaic pael passive participle in Ezra 4:18 and upon rabbinic tradition.[22]

But is "translating" is not the best interpretation. The more viable option states that it "is equally possible that only explanatory interpretation is involved in the present context."[23] That is to say, Ezra and the priests explained and explicated the Word of God. They did not translate it from one language to another, but they read the passage in Hebrew and then exposited it to the people. They were engaging in what we now call "expository preaching."

A word study on פרשׁ is more helpful in ascertaining the meaning than rabbinic tradition and Aramaic stems. Neither tradition nor Aramaic stems should trump what the word actually means. Leslie C. Allen and Timothy S. Laniak agree: "The term also occurs in the Aramaic of Ezra 4:18, but it does not necessarily have the same meaning here."[24] What do the lexicons say? One says that the word means *distinctly declare; make distinct.*[25] *TWOT* says, "The basic meaning still remains, 'to make/be made clear [by revelation, explication, or translation]'" and goes on to say that the word means an "expositor."[26] Lastly, *HALOT* defines the verb as "to separate, distinguish," and mentions the use of its qal infinitive construct form in Leviticus 24:12 ("They put him in custody so that the command of the LORD might be made clear to them") and the only other occurrence of the exact form used in Nehemiah 8:8 (Numbers 15:33–34).[27] Again, the issue is summarized by commentator Derek Kidner, who says, "The basic meaning of the word in question is 'to make distinct or separate,' which could denote either that the reading was well articulated or that the law was read and expounded section by section. Either of these would be appropriate; probably both were true."[28]

Since word study alone cannot determine the true meaning of the word in this particular context, the cultural and biblical contexts must also be examined. The situation and biblical framework bolster the view that Ezra exposited the Scripture. Kidner says of the situation, "Indeed, Nehemiah's indignation at finding families who 'could not speak the language of Judah' on his second visit to Jerusalem about twelve years later, suggests that in his first term of office he could expect Hebrew to be generally understood."[29] Since that was the case, translation would not be needed, but instead the people would need to understand exactly and precisely what God said and what He required. This precise understanding would have to be given by exposition. God's commands needed to be "made clear" by exposition.

Second Chronicles 17 is insightful as it speaks of the Levites' duty to teach the Word and to give what is certainly more than a simple translation from one language to another. They did not simply translate the text. The Bible says,

Then in the third year of his reign he sent his officials, Ben-hail, Obadiah, Zechariah, Nethanel and Micaiah, to teach in the cities of Judah; and with them the Levites, Shemaiah, Nethaniah, Zebadiah, Asahel, Shemiramoth, Jehonathan, Adonijah, Tobijah and Tobadonijah, the Levites; and with them Elishama and Jehoram, the priests. They taught in Judah, having the book of the law of the LORD with them; and they went throughout all the cities of Judah and taught among the people (2 Chronicles 17:7–9).

In summary, word study and a study of the cultural and biblical contexts demonstrate conclusively that Ezra gave an exposition of the Word of God to the people. He helped them understand the Oracles of God. He gave a "periphrastic exposition and application of the law."[30] Jesus knew about this kind of preaching since He was the One spurring Ezra on to do it, and He also knew about it from the incarnational perspective, that is, He was taught the Book of Ezra as a child.

DEUTERONOMY 1:5

The example of Moses in Deuteronomy 1:5 also points to teaching the Bible expositionally. The verse reads,

Across the Jordan in the land of Moab, Moses undertook to expound this law, saying ...

Actually, the whole book of Deuteronomy is an exposition of the Mosaic Law. S.R. Driver confirms this, exclaiming, "the exposition of [the code of the law embodied in Deuteronomy] is the primary object of the discourses which follow. The laws of which this code consists are not, as a rule, stated with abstract, naked brevity; they are accompanied with hortatory introductions and comments; i.e. they are 'expounded' or 'explained.'"[31] Moses' desire was to clearly and completely explain the Mosaic Law to the Israelites. Two verses earlier, in Deuteronomy 1:3, we read, "In the fortieth year, on the first day of the eleventh month, Moses spoke to the children of Israel, according to all that the LORD had commanded him to give to them." Again the stress is upon speaking forth the Word of God and that it is not a matter to be taken lightly.

What does "expound" mean in Deuteronomy 1:5? Peter C. Craigie adroitly answers,

The word expound (*be er*) has the sense of making something absolutely clear or plain; the same verb is used in 27:8 to indicate the clarity or legibility with which the words of the law were to be inscribed in stone ... It is important to stress that the content of Deuteronomy is an exposition of the law ... It is true that there is a common core of law with the earlier books, but here the law is to be explained and applied by Moses to the particular situation of the Israelites.[32]

Lexicons are unanimous in saying that the Hebrew word means "to explain." Other commentators say, "to *explain* ... Here it signifies to expound this law clearly."[33] Another describes this piel perfect verb by saying it means "*make distinct, plain* of letters on tablets; fig. *explain, expound.*"[34] *HALOT* also lists the meaning "elucidate."[35] This is exactly what Moses did. Moses elucidated and explicated the Word of God. Moses was an expository preacher.

Moses did more than simply state facts and figures in a dry, running commentary. J.G. McConville says, "That Moses 'explains' the law emphasizes the concern of Deuteronomy not merely to give information but to teach and persuade."[36] Moses, as a true shepherd, wanted the people to rationally, emotionally, and volitionally grasp and internalize what God had told him. It would lead the people to desire to obey Yahweh. Moses then was to teach and to expound the Word of God while exhorting the Israelites to believe and obey it. This type of teaching should be the model for teaching the Bible. What could be a better model than Moses in Deuteronomy 1:5, where he was to "expound [the] law"? Deuteronomy is thus "'preached law'—that is, law explained with prophetic urgency, divine authority, and a preacher's clarity."[37]

It is not stretching the facts to say that Jesus wanted Moses and Ezra to preach the way they did. Jesus knew the best way to teach the Bible and that way was through expounding it. Both Nehemiah 8 and Deuteronomy 1 give us a snapshot of the preaching that would have delighted Jesus.

Application for preachers, elders, leaders, and Bible teachers

1. MAKE A PLAN TO PREACH THROUGH EVERY BOOK OF THE BIBLE

Are you committed to teach the entire corpus of the Old and New Testaments? Is there any book that you could not preach this Sunday to your people? Assuming you live long enough, do you have a plan to teach from Genesis through Revelation? How about the Song of Solomon? David Hubbard errs when he says, "Preaching on the Song in most congregational settings is difficult. The language is so frank and the theme is so specialized that the messages would probably not minister effectively to the entire church."[38]

On the contrary, all Scripture should be preached because it is all profitable:

All Scripture is inspired by God and profitable for teaching, for reproof, for correction, for training in righteousness; so that the man of God may be adequate, equipped for every good work (2 Timothy 3:16–17).

The Greek word here translated "profitable" means useful, beneficial, or advantageous. Preaching any Bible book helps the congregation and effectively ministers to the entire church.

C.H. Spurgeon was insightful in this area, saying,

No truth is to be kept back ... It is not true that some doctrines are only for the initiated; there is nothing in the Bible which is ashamed of the light ... Cautious reticence is, in nine cases out of ten, cowardly betrayal. The best policy is never to be politic, but to proclaim every atom of the truth so far as God has taught it to you ... All revealed truth in harmonious proportion must be your theme.[39]

2. PREACH THROUGH BOOKS SEQUENTIALLY

There are always exceptions for special services or addressing current events, but the regular fare for the congregation should be verse-by-verse exposition. This assists the preacher in getting the context correct and in preaching all the passages in the Old and New Testaments. In terms of a pattern that has great significance, Paul told the Ephesians that he had discharged all his duty, saying in Acts 20:26–27, "Therefore, I testify to you this day that I am innocent of the blood of all men. For I did not shrink from declaring to you the whole purpose of God." The only way for Paul to accomplish this in three years would have been systematically, expositionally, and book by book. Paul would have agreed with the International Council on Biblical Inerrancy, which stated, "WE AFFIRM that the only type of preaching which sufficiently conveys the divine revelation and its proper application to life is that which faithfully expounds the text of Scripture as the Word of God. WE DENY that the preacher has any message from God apart from the text of Scripture."[40]

As for sequential preaching, Terry Johnson's historical background is helpful:

First, *preach expositorily and sequentially*. When you preach, preach a text of Scripture ... The Reformation can be said to have started for the Reformed churches when in January 1519 Zwingli ... abandoned the lectionary, and began to preach through the book of Matthew ... The abandonment of the *lectio selecta* in favor of the *lectio continua* was an early mark of the Reformed churches and according to Hughes Old, "unquestionably one of the most clear restorations of the form of worship of the early Church." Not only Zwingli, but Luther, Bucer, Oecolampadius, Calvin, the Scottish Reformers, and the English Puritans were all committed to expository, sequential preaching.[41]

3. WHATEVER IS DONE IN A WORSHIP SERVICE, DO NOT LET IT CUT INTO THE SERMON TIME

It is crucial to protect the pulpit. There must be adequate time for the sermon to be delivered thoroughly. Do not let missionary updates, announcements, or music dominate the service, leaving no room for lengthy sermons. If self-control cannot be maintained, move extraneous parts of the service after the sermon or remove them from the service altogether. Robert L. Dabney echoes these sentiments, urging

that the expository method (understood as that which explains extended passages of Scripture in course) be restored to that equal place which it held in the primitive and Reformed Churches; for, first, this is obviously the only natural and efficient way to do that which is the sole legitimate end of preaching, convey the whole message of God to the people.[42]

4. INCLUDE ALL THE COMPONENTS FOR BIBLICAL EXPOSITION

Many differ on the exact number of parts that the expository message must contain. We will look at five aspects that every exposition is obliged to include so that you will honor your Lord and represent His text well.

To start, the man preparing the message must be regenerate and called into the ministry. The godliness of the man preaching cannot be underestimated. The Old Testament designation "man of God" speaks of God's messenger, but also of a man who is holy and specially set apart for the use of the Lord. The expositor is someone whom the Lord has groomed and gifted in His special and providential way. God sovereignly uses the man's unsaved background, his theological training, his family life, and everything about and around him to create a unique vessel for a unique local church.

The second step in the expository process is the preparation. Research and study are nonnegotiables that undergird the systematic proclamation of the Bible. Exegesis, grammatical-historical hermeneutics, and prayer are essential for the pastor to understand exactly what God meant when He inspired the Bible. This extraction process bridges the gaps of history, culture, time, and language found in an ancient book.

The third essential component of the message is the introduction. This is not only an attention-getter or a statement that secures the audience's interest; it must also tell the congregation how the specific passage ties into the overall context. In other words, it connects the passage to the one just before it and gives the hearer a proper foundation to understand the truth. As one said, "In short, expository preaching demands that, by careful analysis of each text within its immediate context and the setting of the book to which it belongs, the full power of modern exegetical and theological scholarship be brought to bear upon our treatment of the Bible."[43]

The fourth step is to actually teach the congregation what God said. The pastor is to expose the congregation to the passage and explain it as he proceeds. This explanation of the original meaning is the bulk of the message. Ideally, each main point is subservient to the central proposition of the text. This is not a running grammar lesson full of super-technical phrases; instead, it is a flowing, comprehendible analysis of any portion of God's Word. The terminology and vocabulary need to be suitable for the majority of the flock to understand and grasp without "dumbing down" any truth. The exegete simply categorizes the raw product, but the expositor arranges the meat on the platter in a well-arranged and beautiful way.

The fifth and final step is what I call the exhortation, or what the Puritans described as pressing the text to the congregation's conscience. Many would use words such as "practical application," or "principlization" to describe this final stage. The preacher persuades, encourages, and calls the congregation either to believe or obey what they have just heard. To use the language of James, the flock must be called to be "doers of the word, and not merely hearers" (James 1:22). Since the preacher is revealing God's Word, he carries all the authority of the Lord Himself. He must exhort the people to be conformed to the likeness of Christ, by the Holy Spirit's power.

Application for laypeople and congregations

1. WHEN YOU LOOK FOR A NEW CHURCH (OR WHEN YOU GO ON VACATION), CALL THE CHURCH AND ASK THEM THIS QUESTION: "WHAT BOOK OF THE BIBLE IS YOUR PASTOR PREACHING THROUGH RIGHT NOW?"

Their answer will tell you the church's view of the Scripture, expository preaching, and much more. It is rare indeed to find a "seeker-sensitive" church preaching though books sequentially.[44] If you are looking online for a church, do not first look at the "Statement of Faith" section (although that is very important); instead, browse the "Sermons Online" section. If you notice a bunch of cute sermon titles without any verses listed, beware. On the other hand, if you see a book of the Bible sequentially listed, the odds are that the church has a high view of Scripture and of preaching.

Capitulation must never be considered when it comes to finding a true, expository preaching church. Heed well the sentiments of a liberal observer, who says, "It is an unusual contradiction that in many churches that claim to be Bible-centered, often using the word Bible in their names, the only Scripture reading in the assembly consists of that brief selection on which the preacher bases the sermon."[45]

2. ENCOURAGE YOUR PASTORAL STAFF TO DO THE HARD WORK OF DIGGING DEEPLY IN THE TREASURES OF SCRIPTURE. THANK THEM FOR FEEDING YOUR SOUL

3. THANK THE LORD FOR GRANTING YOU AND YOUR FAMILY THE GIFT OF A FAITHFUL PASTOR AND LEADERSHIP TEAM

4. READ *BE CAREFUL HOW YOU LISTEN: HOW TO GET THE MOST OUT OF A SERMON* BY JAY ADAMS[46]

Notes

1 **Jerry Vines** and **Jim Shaddix,** *Power in the Pulpit* (Chicago: Moody, 1999), 28.

2 **Ramesh Richard,** *Preparing Expository Sermons* (Grand Rapids: Baker, 2001), 19.

3 **Haddon W. Robinson,** "What is Expository Preaching?" in *Bibliotheca Sacra* 131 (Jan–March 1974), 57.

4 **Richard Mayhue,** "Rediscovering Expository Preaching," in **John MacArthur, Jr.,** and The Master's Seminary Faculty, *Rediscovering Expository Preaching* (Dallas: Word, 1992), 10.

5 **Merrill F. Unger,** *Principles of Expository Preaching* (Grand Rapids: Zondervan, 1955), 33.

6 **Archibald Thomas Robertson,** *Word Pictures in the New Testament*, vol. 2: *Luke* in Quickverse 7.0 (Cedar Rapids, IA: Electronic Edition STEP Files, 1999), note on Luke 4:16.

7 **Marvin R. Vincent,** *Vincent's Word Studies*, vol. 1: *Synoptic Gospels* in Quickverse 7.0 (Cedar Rapids, IA: Electronic Edition STEP Files, 1999), note on Luke 4:17. He says, "The use of these terms by Luke the physician is the more significant from the fact that elsewhere in

the New Testament ἀνοίγω is used for the *opening of a book* (Revelation 5:2–5; 10:2, 8; 20:12); and ἐλίσσω, for *rolling it up* (Revelation 6:14)."

8 Ibid.

9 Albert Barnes, *Barnes' Notes on the New Testament,* Quickverse 7.0 (Cedar Rapids, IA: Electronic Edition STEP Files, 1999), note on Luke 4:21.

10 Vincent, *Word Studies*, note on Luke 4:16.

11 Robert H. Mounce, *The Essential Nature of New Testament Preaching* (Eugene, OR: Wipf & Stock, 1960), 42.

12 F.B. Meyer, *Expository Preaching: Plans and Methods* (London: Hodder & Stoughton, 1910), 78.

13 Mayhue, "Rediscovering Expository Preaching," 11.

14 Alfred Plummer, *The Gospel According to St Luke* (New York: Charles Scribner's Sons, 1898), 556.

15 *Thayer's Lexicon*, s.v. "διερμηνεύω."

16 Joel B. Green, *The Gospel of Luke*, The New International Commentary on the New Testament (Grand Rapids: Eerdmans, 1997), 848.

17 Norval Geldenhuys, *Commentary On The Gospel Of Luke*, The New International Commentary on the New Testament (Grand Rapids: Eerdmans, 1951), 634.

18 Mayhue, "Rediscovering Expository Preaching," 13.

19 H.G.M. Williamson, *Ezra, Nehemiah*, Word Biblical Commentary, vol. 16 (Nashville: Thomas Nelson, 1985), 290–291.

20 F. Charles Fensham, *The Books of Ezra and Nehemiah*, The New International Commentary on the Old Testament (Grand Rapids: Eerdmans, 1982), 217.

21 D.J. Clines, *Ezra, Nehemiah, Esther*, The New Century Bible Commentary (Grand Rapids: Eerdmans, 1984), 184.

22 Edwin Yamauchi, *Ezra–Nehemiah*, The Expositor's Bible Commentary, vol. 4, ed. **Frank E. Gaebelein** (Grand Rapids: Zondervan, 1988), 725. Regarding the Aramaic, Yamauchi says, "Making it clear (*meporas*) translates the Pual participle of the verb *paras*, a form that occurs only here (cf. the Aramaic Pael passive participle *meparas* in Ezra 4:18). Many would derive its meaning from the sense 'to separate,' 'to determine,' hence 'to make clear' (cf. RSV, 'clearly')." He then goes on to discuss Rabbinic tradition, saying, "Rabbinic tradition, however, from the epoch of Rab (AD 175–247) has understood this word as referring to translation from Hebrew into an Aramaic Targum. Thus the Babylonian Talmud (*Megillah* 3a) comments: 'What is meant by the text: And they read in the book, in the law of God, *mephorash*, and gave the sense and caused them to understand the meaning?' And they read in the book, in the Law of God: this indicates the Hebrew text; *mephorash*: this indicates the targum" (see **R. le Deaut,** *Introduction à la Litterature Targuminque* [Rome: Institute Biblique Pontifical, 1966], 23; **M. McNamara,** *Targum and Testament* [Grand Rapids: Eerdmans, 1972], 79–80).

23 Clines, *Ezra, Nehemiah, Esther*, 184.

24 Leslie C. Allen and **Timothy S. Laniak,** *Ezra, Nehemiah, Esther*, New International Biblical Commentary (Peabody, MA: Hendrickson, 2003), 129.

25 Richard Whitaker, *Whitaker's Revised BDB Hebrew–English Lexicon*, 1906 [CD-ROM], in *Bible Works* (Norfolk: BibleWorks LLC, 1992–2003), s.v. "פָּרַשׁ".

26 R. Laird Harris, Gleason L. Archer, Jr., and **Bruce K. Waltke,** *The Theological Wordbook of the Old Testament* (*TWOT*) [CD-ROM] (Chicago: Moody, 1980), in *Bible Works* (Norfolk: BibleWorks LLC, 1992–2003), s.v. "פָּרַשׁ." Interestingly, *TWOT* says, "It is from this Hebrew root that the term 'Pharisee' is derived. The origin both of the movement and the designation itself, Pharisee, is somewhat puzzling. It has been suggested that the Pharisees, under the Hasmonean prince John Hyrcanus (135–104 BC), himself an ex-Pharisee, were expelled from the Sanhedrin and were subsequently branded with the name the 'Perushim,' i.e., 'the separators.' In other words, the term was originally one of opprobrium, akin to that attached to the Holy Club at Oxford, the 'methodists.' And like the Methodists, the Pharisees took the name as their own but used its alternative Hebrew meaning, 'the exponents' (of the Law). The Pharisees are, then, the 'separators' in that they are the expositors of the Law, both written and oral." s.v. "פָּרַשׁ".

27 Ludwig Koehler and **Walter Baumgartner,** *The Hebrew and Aramaic Lexicon of the Old Testament* (*HALOT*) [CD-ROM] (Leiden: Koninklijke Brill NV, 1994–2000), in *Bible Works* (Norfolk: BibleWorks LLC, 1992–2003), s.v. "פָּרַשׁ".

28 Derek Kidner, *Ezra & Nehemiah*, Tyndale Old Testament Commentaries (Downers Grove, IL: InterVarsity Press, 1979), 106–107.

29 Ibid.

30 C.F. Keil and **F. Delitzsch** on Nehemiah 8:1-8, *Commentary on the Old Testament*, vol. 1 [CD-ROM], in *Quickverse* (Omaha: Parsons Church Group, 2000).

31 S.R. Driver, *A Critical and Exegetical Commentary on Deuteronomy*, The International Critical Commentary (New York: Charles Scribner's Sons, 1901), 8–9.

32 Peter C. Craigie, *The Book of Deuteronomy*, The New International Commentary on the Old Testament (Grand Rapids: Eerdmans, 1976), 92. Deuteronomy 27:8 proclaims, "You shall write on the stones all the words of this law very distinctly."

33 Keil and **Delitzsch** on Deuteronomy 1:5, *Commentary on the Old Testament*.

34 Whitaker, *Whitaker's Revised BDB Hebrew–English Lexicon*, s.v. "באר".

35 Koehler and **Baumgartner,** *The Hebrew and Aramaic Lexicon of the Old Testament*, s.v. "באר".

36 J.G. McConville, *Deuteronomy*, Apollos Old Testament Commentary (Downers Grove, IL: InterVarsity Press, 2002), 62.

37 Christopher Wright, *Deuteronomy*, New International Biblical Commentary (Peabody, MA: Hendrickson, 1996), 22.

38 David Hubbard, *Ecclesiastes, Song of Solomon*, Mastering the Old Testament (Dallas: Word, 1991), 260.

39 Charles Haddon Spurgeon, *Lectures To My Students*, vol. 1 (Grand Rapids: Baker, 1977), 77–78.

40 International Council on Biblical Inerrancy, "The Chicago Statement on Biblical Hermeneutics," article 25.

41 Terry Johnson, *The Pastor's Public Ministry* (Greenville: Reformed Academic Press, 2001), 63.

42 Robert L. Dabney, *Sacred Rhetoric* (Edinburgh: Banner of Truth, 1979), 78–79.

43 Greer W. Boyce, "A Plea for Expository Preaching," in *Canadian Journal of Theology* 8 (Jan 1962): 18–19.

44 I have been to a few services in such churches, but a "felt-needs" hermeneutic dominated the sermon series and the biblical interpretation. I even sat through an "exposition" from Amos that was so contorted that the message was not judgment, but "feel good."

45 Fred B. Craddock, *Preaching* (Nashville: Abingdon Press, 1985), 104.

46 Jay E. Adams, *Be Careful How You Listen: How to Get the Most Out of a Sermon* (Birmingham, AL: Solid Ground Christian Books, 2007); original title: *A Consumer's Guide to Preaching* (Wheaton: Victor Books, 1991).

Conclusion

Recently, I visited the Kostnice Church near Prague in the Czech Republic. This church is completely "decorated" with human bones: literally thousands upon thousands of tibias, femurs, and skulls are displayed in ornamental style. There is even a huge candelabrum made from human bones (most of the bones were from people who died from the bubonic plague, although some skeletons were from the Hussite Wars). This ossuary-type of beautification was put in place to assist the congregation. The congregants are to see the bones and then think about their own frailty and mortality. The human bones serve as a wonderful mnemonic to all who walk through the church corridors (and to tourist families).

I desire this book to be a mnemonic of a different sort. I want this book to remind Bible teachers and Bible learners that Jesus is the greatest teacher of all time. I long for Christians to remember that the measure of a man of God lies in his similarity to Jesus (both the life of Christ and His proclamation). This short introduction to the preaching of Jesus has given me refreshment, renewed reverence, and an increased motivation to study the life and message of Christ with a deeper humility and determination.

It will not happen, but I wish the acronym WWJD (What would Jesus do?) would be replaced in homiletical circles with HDJP (How did Jesus preach?). This book is written so that all Christians might embark, or continue their journey, on the lifelong privilege of studying the public proclamation of Jesus.

While this book does not purport to be the definitive study on the preaching of Jesus, it does begin to ask the question, "What could pastors and congregations learn from the style and substance of Jesus' public proclamation?" I applaud the deluge of recent books that promote Christ-centered preaching. Generally, I concur with the authors of these books, because I abhor legalistic preaching full of only "to do" lists. This type of "preaching" is only moralizing, because it spews out command after command but is void of the proclamation of the power of the cross. But in addition to these Christ-centered preaching books, the evangelical church needs a healthy dose of books displaying Jesus' type of preaching.

Furthermore, I rejoice that there is a new interest in the publishing of new and old preaching books, yet only a relative few discuss how congregational members should view preaching. Congregations need to analyze sermons on a better basis than "the pastor seemed to identify with me," "the lecture was upbeat," or "the message made me feel good." When congregations realize that Jesus is the measure of all preaching, that Jesus is the standard for all sermons, and that Jesus Himself is the One with whom all pastors must be compared, then both their worship and ministry expectations will swell to biblical levels. The congregations that love the preaching of Jesus "incarnated" in their pastor will be made up of saints who truly understand and appreciate Bible preaching as it was intended to be by the triune God. May congregations be moved to say in earnest, "My pastor preaches like Jesus!" May the desire of every pastor be: "I want to preach more as my Lord preached."

Instead of calling this a "Conclusion," maybe it would be more aptly titled "Springboard." There cannot be a final conclusion to this work because there is so much more to stay. Here in this book, only a few passages of Jesus' public proclamation have been examined; I hope, therefore, that this book spawns a new generation of books that further examine the preaching of Jesus Christ. I pray that this book inspires a glut of books about the preaching of Jesus, "which if they were written in detail, I suppose that even the world itself would not contain the books that would be written" (John 21:25).

Thankfully, there will never be a "real" conclusion to the study of the preaching of Jesus because I am quite certain that heaven will be replete with more than a symphony of praise unto Jesus Christ. I believe that glorified saints will enjoy the reception of the preaching and teaching of Jesus Himself for all eternity. Heaven will confirm that Jesus is "the Prince of preachers" and the "Preacher of preachers."

Appendix: Recommended reading list for books about worship

Ronald B. Allen, *The Wonder Of Worship* (Nashville: Thomas Nelson, 2001).
Allen gives a five-part examination of worship that is easy to read and very profitable.

Jeremiah Burroughs, *Gospel Worship* (Morgan, PA: Soli Deo Gloria, 1997).
These fourteen Puritan sermons drive the reader to reverently worship God as holy.

D.A. Carson (ed.), *Worship by the Book* (Grand Rapids: Zondervan, 2002).
This book demonstrates that God-honoring worship is not limited by tradition. Carson's chapter is the best and is worth the price of the whole book.

Robert Godfrey, *Pleasing God in Our Worship* (Wheaton: Crossway, 1999).
"Today's Issues" booklets are short and helpful resources. Godfrey introduces the reader to thinking about forms of worship and evaluating worship from God's perspective.

D.G. Hart and John R. Muether, *With Reverence and Awe: Returning to the Basics of Reformed Worship* (Phillipsburg, NJ: Presbyterian & Reformed, 2002).
Read this book if you are interested in the distinguishing characteristics of Reformed worship.

Robert Letham, *Holy Trinity in Scripture, History, Theology, and Worship* (Phillipsburg, NJ: Presbyterian & Reformed, 2005).
Holy Trinity provides a detailed analysis of the triune God that goes way beyond a "data dump." As the title implies, your view of the Trinity is directly related to your worship.

John MacArthur, *The Ultimate Priority* (Chicago: Moody, 1983).
This book is classic MacArthur. It stresses the lifestyle of worship, the object of worship, the consequences of wrong worship, and the blessings of biblical worship.

David Peterson, *Engaging with God: A Biblical Theology of Worship* (Downers Grove: InterVarsity Press, 2002).
Peterson's book yields an exegetically based examination of both the Old and the New Testament passages discussing worship. He gives solid insight into worship from the writings of Paul, John, the writer of Hebrews, and more.

Allen P. Ross, *Recalling the Hope of Glory: Biblical Worship from the Garden to the New Creation* (Grand Rapids: Kregel, 2006).
With detailed precision, Ross inductively lays forth a multitude of biblical passages pertaining to worship.

Books about preaching

Adams, Jay E., *Preaching with Purpose* (Grand Rapids: Zondervan, 1982).

——*Pulpit Speech* (Grand Rapids: Baker, 1971).

As usual, Adam's books are very "user-friendly." He is especially helpful when instructing homiletics students in how to develop applicational outlines.

Azurdia, Arturo G., III, *Spirit Empowered Preaching* (Fearn, Scotland: Christian Focus, 2003).

Azurdia's passion for preaching exudes from this book. Read it and be motivated to see the Holy Spirit instruct your people.

Bickel, R. Bruce, *Light and Heat: The Puritan View of the Pulpit* (Morgan, PA: Soli Deo Gloria, 1999).

The Puritans offer a brilliant example of the primacy of preaching. Bickel demonstrates both the passion and the doctrine of this era of preaching.

Bond, Albert Richmond, *The Master Preacher: A Study of the Homiletics of Jesus* (New York: American Tract Society, 1910).

Although this is an older book examining the preaching of Jesus, there are many gems to be gleaned.

Broadus, John A., *On the Preparation and Delivery of Sermons*, ed. J.B. Weatherspoon (New York: Harper and Row, 1944).

Good preaching books should transcend generations. This book should be read by all students of preaching. Do not let the small font and older stylistic forms scare you away.

Bryson, Harold T., *Expository Preaching: The Art of Preaching Through a Book of the Bible* (Nashville: Broadman & Holman, 1995).

A valuable "how to" preaching book that stresses expository preaching.

Carrick, John, *The Imperative of Preaching* (Carlisle, PA: Banner of Truth, 2002).

This is one of my favorite recent books on preaching. Many are unfamiliar with Carrick's important work on the "indicative and imperative" of preaching.

Chapell, Bryan, *Christ-Centered Preaching* (Grand Rapids: Baker, 1994).

Chapell's book will be seen by future generations as a "classic." His "fallen condition focus" discussion is superb. Every preacher should read this book—*yearly!*

Clowney, Edmund P., *Preaching and Biblical Theology*, (Grand Rapids: Eerdmans, 1961).

——*Preaching Christ in All of Scripture* (Wheaton: Crossway, 2003).

Clowney's books stress the importance of preaching Jesus Christ every time you preach. This commendable goal is taken too far on occasion.

Dabney, R.L., *Evangelical Eloquence* (Carlisle, PA: Banner of Truth, 1999).

Dabney's penchant for long sentences should not stop the mature pastor from reading this classic and benefiting from it.

Select bibliography

Doriani, Daniel M., *Putting the Truth to Work* (Phillipsburg, NJ: Presbyterian & Reformed, 2001).
The most detailed book on biblical application that is in print today.

Eby, David, *Power Preaching for Church Growth* (Fearn, Scotland: Mentor, 1996).
Far from being a seeker-sensitive book, Eby longs for the maturation of the saints through God-honoring preaching.

Fabarez, Michael, *Preaching That Changes Lives* (Nashville: Thomas Nelson, 2002).
A very comprehensive look at biblical preaching. Excellent reminders from a conservative perspective.

Fasol, Al, *A Complete Guide to Sermon Delivery* (Nashville: Broadman & Holman, 1996).
In cookbook-like fashion, Fasol walks through the basics of the art of preaching.

Goldsworthy, Graeme, *Preaching the Whole Bible as Christian Scripture: The Application of Biblical Theology to Expository Preaching* (Grand Rapids: Eerdmans, 2000).
Goldsworthy rightly makes the case that the Old Testament is a Christian book and therefore must be preached as such.

Greidanus, Sidney, *The Modern Preacher and the Ancient Text: Interpreting and Preaching Biblical Literature* (Grand Rapids: Eerdmans, 1988).
Greidanus' strength is teaching the reader to preach Christ from the Old Testament, not from one of the 2700 characters mentioned in the Bible. Watch out for the Lutheran (extreme typology) approach in preaching Christ.

Hegg, David W., *Appointed to Preach* (Fearn, Scotland: Mentor, 1999).
A thorough book discussing the examination, ordination, and appointment of gospel ministers. Should be read by all ordination councils.

Jowett, J.H., *The Preacher, His Life and Work* (London: Hodder and Stoughton, 1912).
I have many disagreements with this work, but it does admirably attempt to observe the preaching style of Jesus.

Kaiser, Walter C., Jr., *Preaching and Teaching from the Old Testament* (Grand Rapids: Baker, 2003).

——*Toward an Exegetical Theology: Biblical Exegesis for Preaching and Teaching* (Grand Rapids: Baker, 1981).
Kaiser marvelously pushes the reader to preach the entire Bible and to preach it so that it accurately conveys authorial intent. Both are must-reads.

Kooienga, William H., *Elements of Style for Preaching* (Grand Rapids: Zondervan, 1989).
This older book attempts to teach the reader to put the "finishing touches" to sermons.

Larsen, David L., *The Anatomy of Preaching: Identifying the Issues in Preaching Today* (Grand Rapids: Kregel, 1999).

A great yet often overlooked book. Larsen is insightful, biblical, and pastoral in his approach. One of my favorites.

Lawson, Steven J., *Famine in the Land* (Chicago: Moody, 2003).

Lawson's enthusiasm comes through his examination of many of the relevant preaching passages in the Bible. You can hear Lawson passionately preach these chapters with firm conviction and biblical clarity.

Lloyd-Jones, D. Martyn, *Preaching and Preachers* (Grand Rapids: Zondervan, 1971).

Maybe the best book on preaching. Re-read this book often for conviction, encouragement, and unique insight from the best theological expositor of the previous generation.

Logan, Samuel T. (ed.), *The Preacher and Preaching* (Phillipsburg, NJ: Presbyterian & Reformed, 1986).

An excellent compilation of essays from a Reformed perspective.

MacArthur, John F., Jr. and **The Master's Seminary Faculty,** *Rediscovering Expository Preaching* (Dallas: Word, 1992).

One of my favorite books on preaching. The faculty of The Master's Seminary offer practical, exegetical, and devotional instruction for expositors of the Text.

McDill, Wayne, *The 12 Essential Skills for Great Preaching* (Nashville: Broadman & Holman, 1994).

McDill is very simple and pastoral. An introductory read from a Southern Baptist.

Meyer, F.B., *Expository Preaching: Plans and Methods* (London: Hodder & Stoughton, 1910).

Meyer's work is dated, but it is interesting to observe his desire for biblical clarity through preaching.

Montoya, Alex, *Preaching with Passion* (Grand Rapids: Kregel, 2000).

This book fills a void in the extremely important topic of passionate preaching. From personal experience, I know this author practices what he writes.

Mounce, Robert H., *The Essential Nature of New Testament Preaching* (Eugene, OR: Wipf & Stock, 1960).

Now republished, Mounce's work on the Greek *kerusso* is invaluable.

Olford, Stephen and **David,** *Anointed Expository Preaching* (Nashville: Broadman & Holman, 1998).

The Olfords' corroboration displays a love for the Word and its proclamation.

Olyott, Stuart, *Preaching: Pure and Simple* (Bryntirion, Wales: Bryntirion Press, 2005).

This work presses the reader for understandable exposition. ***Read it!***

Select bibliography

Perkins, William, *The Art of Prophesying* (Carlisle, PA: Banner of Truth, 1996).
A Puritan classic that has been used by many seminaries over the past few hundred years.

Piper, John, *The Supremacy of God in Preaching* (Grand Rapids: Baker, 1990).
This short book is powerful. You will especially remember (and identify with) Piper's pleas to the Lord before he preaches.

Reymond, Robert L., *The God-Centered Preacher* (Fearn, Scotland: Mentor, 2003).
Reymond's "The Need for a God-centered pulpit" chapter is excellent.

Richard, Ramesh, *Preparing Expository Sermons* (Grand Rapids: Baker, 2001).
A very basic book on expository preaching (a good thing). Its cookbook-like instruction makes it beneficial to those in their beginning stages of preaching. A good book to give to your leadership as they teach more often.

Robinson, Haddon W., *Biblical Preaching* (2nd ed.) (Grand Rapids: Baker Academic, 1980, 2001).
——*Making a Difference in Preaching* (Grand Rapids: Baker, 1999).
Robinson has written some gold standards in expository preaching. Read his older books that stress expository preaching by men.

Sangster, W.E., *Power in Preaching* (London: Epworth Press, 1958).
Sangster's work ties power directly to the Word.

Scharf, Greg, *Prepared to Preach* (Fearn, Scotland: Mentor, 2005).
A good description of the preacher's preparation is included.

Shaddix, Jim, *The Passion Driven Sermon* (Nashville: Broadman & Holman, 2003).
Shaddix's work should be read alongside Montoya's.

Spurgeon, Charles H., *Lectures to My Students* (Grand Rapids: Baker, reprinted 1977).
A great work emphasizing more than just the content and the art of preaching. Top ten.

Stewart, James, *Heralds of God* (Grand Rapids: Baker, reprinted 1971).

Stott, John, *Between Two Worlds: The Art of Preaching in the Twentieth Century* (Grand Rapids: Eerdmans, 1982).
——*The Preacher's Portrait* (London: Billing & Sons, 1961).
It is rare to find one author who can contribute two classic books on preaching, but Stott has done exactly that. Both of these works are simply excellent and should be read—and re-read.

Thompson, William D., *Preaching Biblically Exegesis and Interpretation* (Nashville: Abingdon Press, 1981).

Unger, Merrill F., *Principles of Expository Preaching* (Grand Rapids: Zondervan, 1955).
An older work that still offers valid insight.

Vines, Jerry, and **Shaddix, Jim,** *Power in the Pulpit* (Chicago: Moody, 1999).
A comprehensive look at preaching. The authors instruct preachers in every imaginable subject related to homiletics.

York, Hershael, and **Decker, Bert,** *Preaching with Bold Assurance: A Solid and Enduring Approach to Engaging Exposition* (Nashville: Broadman & Holman, 2003).
An excellent resource for developing the fine aspects of preaching. Especially impressive is the "eye communication" section. Make sure you read this book.

Articles about preaching

Boyce, Greer, W., "A Plea for Expository Preaching," in *Canadian Journal of Theology* 8 (Jan 1962), 12–21.

Bugg, Charles, "Back to the Bible: Toward a New Description of Expository Preaching," in *Review And Expositor* 90 (1993), 413–421.

Carson, D.A., "Accept No Substitutes," in *Leadership* 17/3 (1996), 87–88.

Chapell, Bryan, "Components of Expository Preaching," in *Preaching,* 10 (May–June 1995), 4–11.

Kaiser, Walter C., "The Crisis in Expository Preaching Today," in *Preaching,* vol. 11 (Sept–Oct 1995), 4–12.

Lawson, Steven J., "The Pattern of Biblical Preaching: An Expository Study of Ezra 7:10 and Nehemiah 8:1-18," in *Bibliotheca Sacra* 158/632 (Oct–Dec 2001), 451–466.

Robinson, Haddon W., "The Heresy of Application," in *Leadership Magazine* (Fall 1997), 21–27.

——"What is Expository Preaching?" in *Bibliotheca Sacra* 131 (Jan–March 1974), 55–60.

Vines, Jerry, and **Allen, David,** "Hermeneutics, Exegesis, and Proclamation," in *Criswell Theological Review* 1/2 (Spring 1987), 309–334.

York, Hershael W., and **Blue, Scott A.,** "Is Application Necessary in the Expository Sermon?" in *Southern Baptist Journal of Theology* 3/2 (Summer 1999), 70–84.

About Day One:

Day One's threefold commitment:

- To be faithful to the Bible, God's inerrant, infallible Word;
- To be relevant to our modern generation;
- To be excellent in our publication standards.

I continue to be thankful for the publications of Day One. They are biblical; they have sound theology; and they are relative to the issues at hand. The material is condensed and manageable while, at the same time, being complete—a challenging balance to find. We are happy in our ministry to make use of these excellent publications.

JOHN MACARTHUR, PASTOR-TEACHER, GRACE COMMUNITY CHURCH, CALIFORNIA

It is a great encouragement to see Day One making such excellent progress. Their publications are always biblical, accessible and attractively produced, with no compromise on quality. Long may their progress continue and increase!

JOHN BLANCHARD, AUTHOR, EVANGELIST AND APOLOGIST

Visit our website for more information and to request a free catalogue of our books.

www.dayone.co.uk

ANDY MCINTOSH

208 PAGES PAPERBACK

978–1–903087–15–2

Andy McIntosh is a scientist who sees no contradiction between the science he writes and lectures about, and the events of creation described in the book of Genesis. He believes that all Christian doctrine, directly or indirectly, is founded in the literal events of the first eleven chapters of the Bible, and that these 'foundations' of the faith have been undermined in the church by the fallible theories of evolution.

A valuable addition to the Creation versus Evolution debate.

Andy McIntosh, DSc, FIMA, CMath, FEI, CEng, FInstP, MIGEM, FRAeS is Professor of Thermodynamics and Combustion Theory at the University of Leeds. He has had a career spanning thirty years of conducting scientific research in mathematics, combustion and aeronautics both in academia and government establishments. He is married with three children and speaks regularly both in the UK and abroad concerning the importance of origins. Latterly, his research has brought in the life sciences with the study of the bombardier beetle, and the whole field of biomimetics—learning engineering solutions from nature.

Genesis for today

Showing the relevance of the Creation/Evolution debate to today's society

'Genesis IS for today'—JOHN MACARTHUR

WITH NEW CHAPTER: 'GENESIS AND THE 21ST CENTURY'

'This is an excellent book for all to read and to give as a gift to interested sceptics.'
EVANGELICAL TIMES

'For those who have eyes to see, here is ample proof that God's revealed truth is as trustworthy as ever—and infinitely more certain than every human speculation.'
JOHN MACARTHUR

He made the stars also:
What the Bible says about the stars

STUART BURGESS

192PP, ILLUSTRATED PAPERBACK

ISBN 978–1–903087–13–8

This book teaches clearly and biblically the purpose of the stars and the question of extra-terrestrial life. Dr Burgess explains how the earth has a unique purpose in supporting life and how the stars have a singular purpose in shining light on it. He explains why the universe contains such natural beauty and how the stars reveal God's character.

Dr Stuart Burgess is Head of Department of Mechanical Engineering at the University of Bristol. His research areas include the study of design in nature. He previously worked in industry, designing rocket and satellite systems for the European Space Agency. He is winner of the Worshipful Company of Turners Gold Medal for the design of the solar array deployment system on the £1·4 billion ENVISAT earth observation satellite.

'Dr Burgess has a very clear style and his book brims with interesting material. It will be greatly appreciated.'
—*DR PETER MASTERS, METROPOLITAN TABERNACLE*

PAUL TAYLOR

160PP, ILLUSTRATED PAPERBACK

ISBN 978–1–84625–071–2

Truth, lies and Science education

Paul Taylor

Most of us are totally unaware of what actually goes on in the teaching environment in the classroom. We may attend parents' evenings and discuss with the teacher the progress of our children in the classroom. We help with (and sometimes actually do) our children's homework. Parents and grandparents will talk with their children and grandchildren about what they are taught, but the children are unable to explain why they are taught what they are taught or what are the philosophical ideologies behind the teaching. In this carefully researched book, Paul Taylor powerfully and devastatingly brings to light the underlying thinking that is the basis for so much of what is taught in our modern schools.

I can warmly commend this book to everyone that has an interest in the education of our young people.
DR A J MONTY WHITE,
CHIEF EXECUTIVE, ANSWERS IN GENESIS

Students spend more time with their teachers/professors than they do with their parents in learning to understand what life is all about. As a result, their formalized education has a great impact on their worldview. Truth, Lies and Science Education is a valiant attempt to tackle this issue head on to engage the education system and parents in understanding the realities of what is being taught to children and how they are being conformed to a secular way of thinking about every aspect of reality.
KEN HAM,
PRESIDENT OF ANSWERS IN GENESIS, USA

God's prescription for a healthy marriage

ANDREW OLIVER

160PP, ILLUSTRATED PAPERBACK

ISBN 978–1–84625–095–8

The family is under threat. Contemporary culture and changes in legislation are seeking to redefine its structure, parents are increasingly giving over to the state the responsibility of disciplining their children, and homes are constantly bombarded by immoral images of the 'family' through TV. The great need today is to return to biblical principles for family life. The Bible is God's manual for the people he created in his image, and therefore it has much to say on this crucial issue. Here, Andy Oliver guides us helpfully through the biblical teaching on marriage and family life, and emphasizes the need to follow God's Word if we are to build solid foundations for a healthy family.

Andy Oliver comes from Northern Ireland, where he ran his own small business before entering full-time Christian ministry. He is engaged in missionary service and pastoral ministry in Albania, and he is a frequent speaker at university student meetings on behalf of BSKSH (IFES Albania). He and his wife, Ela, have two daughters, Rakela and Emma, and a son, Jack.

Across Europe, and, indeed, the Western world, the crisis in marriage and family life is impacting Christian and non-Christian alike, and Andy Oliver's book provides a timely reminder of God's good purposes for us. His approach is thought-provoking and uncompromising and, while you might not agree with every application, you will benefit greatly from this refreshingly direct and practical introduction to what the Bible teaches.

JONATHAN LAMB, AUTHOR, DIRECTOR OF LANGHAM PREACHING (LANGHAM PARTNERSHIP INTERNATIONAL) AND FORMER ASSOCIATE GENERAL SECRETARY OF IFES